THE WOMEN'S BOOK OF RACQUETBALL

SHANNON WRIGHT
WITH STEVE KEELEY

Contemporary Books, Inc.
Chicago

Library of Congress Cataloging in Publication Data

Wright, Shannon.
  The women's book of racquetball.

  Includes index.
  1. Racquetball.   2. Sports for women.
I. Keeley, Steve, joint author.   II. Title.
GV1017.R3W74   796.34'3   80-65927
ISBN 0-8092-7066-8
ISBN 0-8092-7064-1 (pbk.)

Cover photo: Art Shay

Instructional photos: Tim Yost and Mike Zeitman

Text photos: Davey Bledsoe, Kip Brundage, Sue Capiel, Carole Charfauros, Coors All-Pro, Ektelon, Lou Giampetroni, Henderson Design, Junebug Photography, Leach Industries, Gene McElroy, National Racquetball Club, Ray Oram, Dave Northcutt, Phillips Organization, Clay Scott, Art Shay, Jim Schatz, Phil Stepp, Chuck Weed, Steve Wells, Tim Yost, Mike Zeitman

Copyright © 1980 by Service Press Inc. and Wright Racquetball Inc.
All rights reserved
Published by Contemporary Books, Inc.
180 North Michigan Avenue, Chicago, Illinois 60601
Manufactured in the United States of America
Library of Congress Catalog Card Number: 80-65927
International Standard Book Number: 0-8092-7066-8 (cloth)
                                                    0-8092-7064-1 (paper)

Published simultaneously in Canada by
Beaverbooks
953 Dillingham Road
Pickering, Ontario L1W 1Z7
Canada

Contents

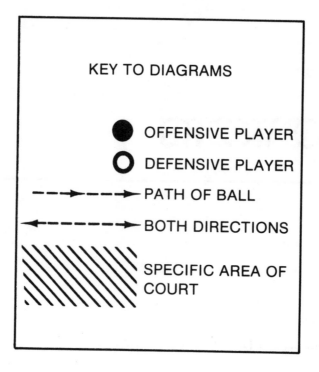

KEY TO DIAGRAMS

● OFFENSIVE PLAYER

○ DEFENSIVE PLAYER

PATH OF BALL

BOTH DIRECTIONS

SPECIFIC AREA OF COURT

NOTE TO LEFT-HANDED PLAYERS

The following material is worded for right-handed players. Left-handers should read the word *right* as *left,* and vice versa, to follow the instruction correctly.

Foreword

You are going to learn racquetball from this book like you've never learned it before. The reason? Well, there are two reasons, and their names are Shannon Wright and Steve Keeley.

Shannon is the best female player in the history of the game. She won the 1977 and 1978 national singles championships and is the NRC professional tour's all-time top female money winner. When people talk about women's racquetball, you know they're talking about Shannon Wright. And everyone who has taken a racquet into hand with purpose has heard of Shannon's co-author, Steve Keeley. Steve has been one of the top male professionals since I established racquetball's first pro tour in 1973. Perhaps more significant to you, he is the most respected instructor and author in the sport. His

Complete Book of Racquetball, up until now, has been the game's bible. (Now, of course, the ladies have their own bible in *The Women's Book of Racquetball*.) Plus, just look at Steve's *It's a Racquet!*, *The Kill & Rekill Gang*, and *Racquetball Lessons Made Easy* to see what an articulate and thorough instructor he is. So there you have them: the game's premiere woman player and its foremost author-instructor.

But why not judge these two by this book? In glancing through the galleys and page proofs, I'd have to say that this text is even more complete than *The Complete Book of Racquetball*. Now, before Steve Keeley creases my handball-pocked dome with an overhead, let me explain.

First, the photos in this book are the best ever to appear in any racquetball book. Next, the diagrams are not your run-of-the-court *Xs, Os,* and dotted lines. No, these graphics are much more detailed and much more informative—just glance through the book to verify this. Then, the "test yourself" sections are terrific instructional fun. Finally—I've saved the best for last—the picture captions. I'm not kidding! Just look at any of the tournament action photos, or any of the sequence instructional photos, or any of the photos in the beautiful opening pictorial of Shannon Wright playing Janell Marriott. You've never seen such detailed captions in any sports book. All this adds up to just what I said—the most complete racquetball text yet.

My thanks to Shannon and Steve for the opportunity to write this foreword. They have allowed me the occasion to expound on their book and on women in racquetball. So far it's been a short, yet explosive, history . . . and there's a long and sensational story to come. Did you know that *you* and *The Women's Book of Racquetball* are important ingredients in that story? It's a fact, and it's fortunate that you ladies and this "bible" came along at the same time.

But what about us deprived male racquetballers? Well, I can only speak for myself, but I'll take on any lady player—just give me twenty points, the serve, and *The Women's Book of Racquetball!*

Bob Kendler
Founder and President,
National Racquetball
Club and the United States
Racquetball Association

Bob Kendler, president of the National Racquetball Club and United States Racquetball Association. (NRC)

Portrait of a Professional Match

Janell and I battle it out on the court again. This is the first game of our semifinals match at the pro stop in Southfield, Michigan. This photo offers a lesson in the rules. There are two ways to avoid an opponent's shot and thus escape an avoidable hinder. You can either go out of the way or go way *up* out of the way. Here, Janell chooses the latter method. (Portrait photos by Bledsoe.)

My basic game plan going into the match against Janell is to *serve and shoot*. This is sometimes called the *big game* or *power* racquetball. I am serving well in the first game and eliciting many weak service returns. Here I capitalize on such a return by using proper shot strategy with basic backhand flair. My stroke is spastic at best, but fortunately my shot selection is perfect—a backhand kill into the backhand corner. I say that my choice of shots is correct because (1) the ball should be *killed* because of our relative court positions (I'm in front of Janell), (2) this ball should be placed low into the *left corner* because I'm taking the shot with my backhand on the left side of the court.

I like to give my racquet partial credit for my shot making. In this picture you get a clear view of both of our racquets. I don't know about Janell's, but mine is fairly head-light for more head speed, flexible for more power, and strung loosely for more control.

Let's scrutinize the situation in this photo from the standpoints of the stroke and the shot. Strokewise, my backhand is more technically correct than in the previous picture—probably because my location deeper in the court allowed me more time to set up on the shot. Note that I've just hit the ball and my body weight is transferred almost entirely to my lead foot. Much of this proper weight transfer from back to front foot was precipitated earlier in the stroke by my shoulders and hips opening forcefully with the swing toward the front wall.

Positionwise, the choice of shots is also correct. Here, strategy dictates that the ball be pinched (killed, hitting the side wall before the front wall) into the left front corner. The reasons: (1) I'm contacting the ball below my knees, so it should be hit offensively; (2) my station in the center of the court (not to mention that this time Janell didn't go way *up* out of my way) demands that I kill the ball into the side wall first rather than straight into the front wall.

Besides serve and shoot, my game plan whenever I play Janell calls for consistency. Consistency has two components: mental execution and physical execution. This means that every time I get an easy setup such as this one, I must execute it with robot efficiency—no mind or body errors.

The robot in me really came out here in the first game: (1) I made few mental errors in taking the right shots from the right court positions: (2) I made few physical errors in hitting the ball solidly with my grooved stroke. Note again in this photo that most backhand below-the-knee setups on the left side in the front court should be killed into the front backhand corner.

This photo offers a study of "improper" shot selection as well as proper anticipation. My backhand is so grooved at this tournament that at times I attempt some fairly illogical shots. Here, I'm ripping a chest-high setup for a kill attempt into my favorite left front corner. That's wrong. Shots such as this presented above the waist and in deep court should be returned with a pass or ceiling ball, preferably the latter.

Janell is anticipating the shot well here in two respects: (1) Looking back as the opponent sets up. A photo taken a split second before this one would reveal that Janell watched me until just before I contacted the ball. Then she turned her head toward the front wall to pick up the ball's flight. (P.S.: It's much safer to look back if you wear eyeguards.) (2) Standing correctly as the opponent sets up. Janell is positioned correctly in an open stance. That is, her feet are placed as if in imaginary starting blocks—ready for a quick push off forward.

My two-pronged game plan of serve-and-shoot plus robot efficiency worked well the first game to the tune of a 21-4 rout. The forehand stroke is usually the mainstay of any serve-and-shoot game, and mine is no exception—at least it wasn't during this opening game. Here's a forehand worth bragging about, instructionally speaking: (1) The height of ball contact is ideally just below my knees, away from my body and midline deep in my stance. (2) My footwork in this instance is exemplary. My front foot steps across into a closed stance, which initiates weight transfer from rear to front foot. (3) My wrist snaps just before the instant I hit the ball. This wrist pop increases racquet head speed (notice the racquet blur), which translates into a high-velocity smasheroo.

It would all be so divine if only I were watching the ball instead of looking at where the ball is going.

A further lesson in eye contract, in regard to eye-guards and glass courts: First, eyeguards present no visual hindrance. The style I'm wearing here is regular glasses, except the lenses are not prescription—they protect the eyes rather than aid vision. Second, glass courts do take some getting used to. Eye contact on the swing is especially important on a three-wall glass court in which only the front wall is solid. The dark ball melts into the dark walls unless you really concentrate. This particular exhibition court in Southfield has one big visual advantage over most of the fish bowls I play in. Look closely and you'll see thin vertical lines ex-tending from the floor to about three feet up the two side and back glass walls. These don't limit gallery viewing from the outside, yet they provide a semisolid background for the players within which the ball zooms around no more than three feet off the floor most of the time.

By the way, I probably missed my kill-shot attempt in this photo. The angle of the racquet at the moment of contact is too far upward and too underhanded, which no doubt will cause the ball to shoot too high off the strings.

Second-game action. Heck, the first was such a cake-walk that I haven't even bothered to remove my warm-up bottoms—which I usually do midway through the opening game. However, I did change my glove because when my grip starts to slip even slightly the best strokes in the world are to no avail.

I discovered back in the first game that my drive serve to the backhand side gave Janell fits. I'm continuing to badger her with it in this game, resorting to a hard Z-serve to her backhand only on my second "safe" serve after a short serve. I never experiment with my service or shot selection in an important match since it's so easy to lose momentum. (The time for trial-and-error testing is in practice *before* the tourney.) Thus, adhering to the old sports adage, "Never change a winning game," I came out serving and shooting in the second. Here, you see me hitting the only logical shot off one of Janell's weak returns—a kill into the right front corner. Notice that Janell is located directly behind me so that I don't know on which side she'll come around my body in an attempt to cover my shot. For this reason, I'm aiming right at a one-foot-square imaginary box in the right front corner. That is, front wall (straight-in kill) or side wall (pinch kill) initial contact on the kill is a moot matter—as long as the ball stays low.

This is similar to the last photo with one positional difference. Can you spot it? Here, I can feel, or sense, Janell coming around the left side of my body to cover my kill. I have the two usual choices of kill shots: straight in or side wall first. A side wall pinch kill in this instance would bring the ball scooting around into the middle of the court, which is where Janell will be in a split second. In other words, my kill shot would have to be an absolute roll-off to be a winner. Not smart! Instead, I opt here for the straight-in kill, which hits the front wall first and carries out of reach down the right side wall. This allows a greater margin of error on my shot.

Note in this and the previous photo that my stance on the stroke is relatively upright. (Nonetheless, I've contacted the ball below my knees.) Contrary to racquetball's early school of misthought, when you kill the ball it isn't necessary to crouch deeply at the knees and bend way over at the waist like a chimpanzee in the attack mode of locomotion. All that is nice to do if you have time, but the speeding sphere often precludes such conveniences.

"Hinder ball!" is the call. Janell and I constantly hip and elbow our way into that important center court position. Don't get me wrong—we do usually give each other plenty of room to swing, but we refuse to budge beyond that. In this case, Janell has just blasted a forehand pass that rebounded past her left knee. All I see are legs—no ball—and I barely get my racquet on the eclipsed sphere. My hindering opponent isn't blocking the play intentionally, so only an unavoidable hinder is called. That is, play simply goes over with no penalty point.

This and other photos in this section portray the torturous life of the racquetball tennis shoe—skidding, scuffing, slapping, and scraping. It's no wonder that your court boots rank right up there in equipment importance with the racquet and eyeguards. Don't skimp on shoes or you'll be sorry. Besides hinders and shoes, this picture offers little other instruction. My stroke is reprehensible, but my excuse is, "You can't hit what you can't see."

Steve Keeley postulates in his offensive theory of play that on an advanced skill level the offensive player consistently drubs the defensive player. To wit, the shooter has it over the countershot maker. Therefore, the theory goes, you should: (1) take the most offensive shot (a kill) whenever possible—for example, when returning a knee-high setup in front court; (2) take the next most offensive shot possible (a pass) when it isn't reasonable to go for the kill—for example, when returning a waist-high setup in deep court; (3) and take the least offensive shot (actually a defensive shot, which is almost always a ceiling ball) when it isn't feasible to go for the kill or pass. An example of this last point is in this photo—when you are off balance with your head tucked into your armpit like an antisocial flamingo, with your legs stretched apart like a gawky giraffe doing a split. Here you see me, the racquet-wielding flamingo-giraffe hybrid, scrambling to hit a ceiling ball to neutralize my awkward position.

This photo also displays one instance in which the extra long rather than the standard length racquet would be advantageous for that extra inch of reach. Still, I prefer to use the standard length of racquet because its decreased weight and length mean I can get greater racquet head speed on my swing. This translates into increased power. You should try out both lengths to determine your preference.

I am often my worst opponent on the court. Typically, I trounce my rival in the first game, jump off to an ostensibly insurmountable lead in the second, and then stop trying. Seventeen is my hex number at which I let up. Once I get over the psychological hump at seventeen points my confidence soars. But, until then, my momentum motor idles.

Here, I lead 17–6 in the second game against Janell. It should be all over but, yep, it's not-so-sweet seventeen again. This photo tells it all: this is no way to hit a shot, even if I am off balance. You can see that the swing intensity and wrist pop on the stroke aren't there. I'm dumping the ball rather than pounding it into the corner. It doesn't take any crystal racquetball to foresee that I'm going to lose this point when Janell powders my blooping kill attempt, and I'm going to keep losing points until I stop patty caking the ball.

Janell ran ten straight points before I got off my hex number for the eighteenth point. That made it 18–16, my lead. Apparently close but, as I say, my confidence soars with only three points to go. I reinstituted my original game plan—the *big game* of serve and shoot—and got two quick points. So it was 20–16 and I needed just one more good serve.

In this photo I have just hit match point serve, a power drive left which has earned me this midcourt setup. Note that my backhand here has focus—an intensity of effort at that split second of ball-on-string contact. It's similar to the focus of a karate punch at the instant of fist-on-flesh contact. The stroke focus is there and so is the shot selection. Here the ball is below my knees, which means that the offensive theory of play clicks in my subconscious. My mind signals my body to go for it—kill the ball. Fine, but where to kill it? This match point photo illustrates an uncommon situation: a backhand setup on the forehand side of the court. A kill shot rule of thumb filters through my subconscious and down to my racquet arm. It says, "shoot into the nearest corner"—in this case the right front corner. I do, and it rolls. The final score is 21–4, 21–16.

1
The Game

Frozen in an instant of intense concentration, 1979 national champ Karin Walton sets for the kill against Janell Marriott. Note the shoulder rotation and the high forehand backswing. (Charfauros)

One reason racquetball has bounced to the top as one of the nation's most popular leisure sports is the simplicity of the game. I teach my absolute greenhorn students the rules during just the first fifteen minutes of our initial lesson. The same rules can be learned in just as brief a time from reading an overview of the sport's fundamentals. Let's look at such an overview now, remembering that this is only a simplistic review intended to enable you to start swinging. See Appendix C in the back of this book for the complete official regulations. In addition to the overview and complete rules, I have prepared a self-evaluation quiz, which appears at the end of this chapter. Use this quick quiz as a learning aid and to make sure you—and your court buddies—are ready to hit the hardwood.

Eight-man doubles? No, four are mere shadows cast by sweaty bodies under the Southern California sun. There, outdoor three-wall doubles is a popular variety of the sport. (Northcutt)

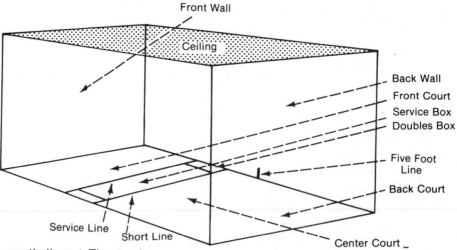

Anatomy of the four-wall racquetball court. The standard twenty-by-twenty-by-forty-foot indoor court has the volume capacity (to hold perspiration) of a large swimming pool.

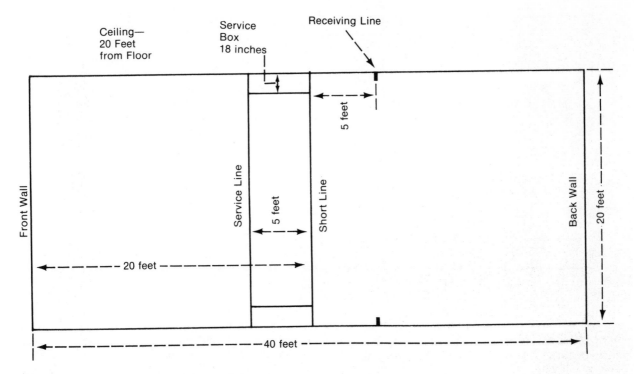

Schematic layout of the court floor. This is what a racquetball court looks like when you jump up for a ceiling shot and get stuck to the ceiling. The twenty-by-forty-foot floor seems like a vast, unfamiliar territory to the beginning player, but the area seems to shrink as you become more experienced.

THE BASICS

Racquetball may be played indoors or outdoors, though the indoor game is considered the standard. Our sport takes one of three forms, depending on the number of participants: singles, cutthroat, or doubles. The most popular game is singles, in which two players compete. In cutthroat three players take part, with one player serving, scoring, and playing against the other two as a team. In doubles four players participate, two on each team.

The combat arena for racquetball is a twenty-by-twenty-by-forty-foot boxlike court consisting of four walls, a ceiling, and a floor. All six of these surfaces are used during a game. The only markings on the court delineate a service box in the middle of the floor and two "five-foot lines," five feet behind the service box. These latter two lines keep the service receiver from charging serves and decapitating the server with her racquet.

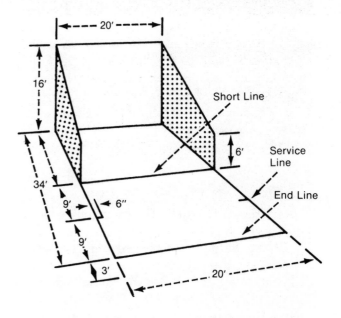

Outdoor play on the three-wall court provides sweet-smelling racquetball perfume consisting of these ingredients: sun, sweat, and burning rubber.

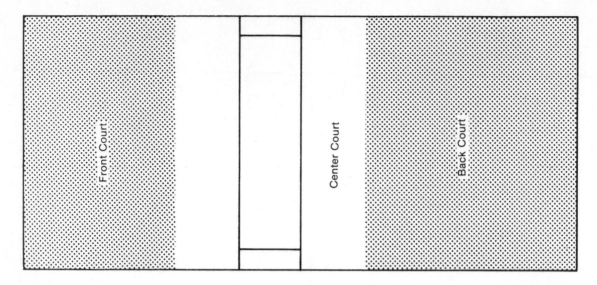

For purposes of instruction and for simplification, the court is often divided into three areas: back court, center court, and front court. Your location on the court while setting up for a shot is one way of strategically determining your choice of shots. Shots in front court are usually hit offensively—a kill. Shots in center court are also handled aggressively—a kill or pass. Shots in back court should be hit less offensively by all but advanced players—a pass or ceiling ball.

The game's basic format is simple. The server serves the ball, the returner returns it, and a rally ensues. In this rally the two singles players (or teams in doubles) alternately hit the ball, striving to outmaneuver each other to win points. This outmaneuvering involves stroke control, stroke power, hustle, strategy, and gamesmanship. Still, for the novice as well as the professional, all this boils down to hitting the ball low on the front wall away from the opponent.

The game is conveniently divided into four parts: serve, serve return, rally, and error. Let's examine each of these.

Serve

The server initiates play by standing within the service box, bouncing the ball once on the floor and hitting it to the receiver. The served ball must travel directly to the front wall. If it contacts the floor, ceiling, or sidewall first, the server loses her serve. After front wall contact, the served ball must travel toward rear court and bounce on the floor between the short line and the back wall. Though the serve must strike the front wall initially, it may hit one of the sidewalls (but not the ceiling or both sidewalls on the fly) en route to its first floor bounce.

The server gets two chances, or faults, to get the ball into play legally. Examples of faults include a short serve, in which the served ball doesn't carry beyond the short line; a long serve, in which the served ball carries from the front to the back wall on the fly; a foot fault, in which the server steps outside the service box during the serve; and breaking the ten-second rule by taking more than ten seconds to serve. Two faults in a row result in a loss of the serve.

Serve Return

After the serve the receiver simply returns the served ball to the front wall. This return must be made before the served ball bounces twice on the floor. Note that the receiver is allowed to hit her serve return on the fly—before any floor bounce at all—as long as this fly return occurs behind the five-foot lines. The serve return may hit any combination of walls and/or the ceiling en route to the front wall. The only stipulation is that the serve return must hit the front wall before touching the floor.

Rally

The rally follows the serve and serve return. This is the guts of the game, during which the

Perennial national champ Marty Hogan is a former high school gymnast and tumbler. Here he takes to the air to avoid a ball welt on the back of his leg. (Charfauros)

two singles players, or the two doubles teams, alternate hitting the ball to the front wall until one of them commits a hitting error. The regulations governing shots during the rally are basically the same as those for the serve return. Each shot may be hit either after the first floor bounce or on the fly. On these shots the ball may contact any combination of walls, including the ceiling, as long as it makes it to the front wall before touching the floor. Hence, racquetball consists of the serve, the serve return, and the rally.

Error

The take-a-turn rally continues until one of the two players or teams makes an error. An error may occur in one of two ways: (1) One player lets the ball bounce twice on the floor during the rally before she makes the return to the front wall. This is called a *double bounce*, and it ends the rally. (2) One of the player's, or team's, shots hits the floor en route to the front wall. This is termed a *skip ball*, and it also ends the rally. An error in either of the above instances results in either a point for the server, or a side-out for the receiver. I'll explain these terms next.

Serve, return, rally, and error—that, plus sweat, is racquetball. And it leads us to the game's point scoring system. The server scores a point when her opponent makes an error, as in the cases I just described. Only the server wins points. The receiver wins a side-out rather than a point when her opponent errors first during the rally. This side-out means that the server and receiver change positions, with the new server gaining the right to win a point on the

You won't know what's happening behind you unless you glance back when your opponent hits the ball. (Zeitman)

SELF-EVALUATION QUIZ

(For answers and scoring evaluation, see Appendix A.)

1. The most popular game of racquetball is: (a) singles, (b) doubles, or (c) cutthroat.
2. True or false: The served ball may hit the ceiling first, as long as it next hits the front wall.
3. True or false: The served ball, after its front wall contact, must hit the floor between the service line and the back wall.
4. The serve return may be taken: (a) after the first bounce, (b) after the second bounce, (c) before any bounce, (d) both a and c, or (e) a, b, and c.
5. True or false: In cutthroat, only the serve returner scores points.
6. True or false: The serve return must travel directly to the front wall, after which it may hit any combination of walls or the ceiling.

One form of the unavoidable or unintentional hinder is the backswing hinder. In this situation the player swinging holds up if she senses her opponent is close behind. Play goes over. (Zeitman)

next rally. These exchanges of position by the server and receiver continue as the two players accumulate points on the serve. The first one to twenty-one points wins the game. Note that if the score ties at 20-20, there is no need to win by two points, as in Ping-Pong. In racquetball, the winner of the next point takes the game by a 21-20 margin. The best two out of three games makes up a match, which is the whole shebang. This means that a player may win a match either by taking two straight games or by losing only one game out of three. An abbreviated third game called a *tie breaker* is popular nowadays. The tie breaker is played to eleven points and, again, there is no need to win by two points.

That's racquetball. You can call it four-walled tennis plus perspiration, or just sweaty chess with footwork. Whatever, it all adds up to healthy fun. Now try the rule quiz.

7. One of two things may happen when one player makes an error during a rally. What are these two things?
8. Is a 21-20 final game score possible?
9. True or false: A foot fault occurs when the server steps on one of the lines of the service box.
10. True or false: A side-out means the receiver wins a point and the right to serve.
11. What does hitting the ball on the fly mean?
12. How much time does the server have to serve?
13. True or false: The served ball may legally hit two sidewalls on the fly.
14. The tie breaker third game is usually played to how many points?
15. Shots during the rally may be hit: (a) after the first bounce, (b) after the second bounce, (c) before any bounce, (d) both a and c, or (e) a, b, and c.
16. What happens if the serve hits the sidewall before the front wall?

17. How many chances or faults does the server get to put the ball into play legally?
18. True or false: The served ball, after hitting the front wall, may legally hit a sidewall before the floor bounce.
19. There are many ways to fault during the serve. Name two of them.
20. How many players participate in doubles?
21. A match may consist of: (a) one game, (b) two games, (c) three games, (d) both a and b, or (e) both b and c.
22. Give the dimensions of a regulation four-wall racquetball court.
23. The serve may be hit after the server bounces the ball on the floor; (a) no times, (b) one time, (c) two times, (d) both a and b, or (e) both b and c.
24. Is a 22-20 final game score possible?
25. In singles, the player who may score points is: (a) the server, (b) the receiver, (c) both a and b, or (d) none of the above.

Peggy Steding through the peephole. Steding was the first dominant female player in racquetball's history. She was invincible in the early 1970s, winning the national singles title in 1973, 1974, 1975, and 1976. (Zeitman)

Keeley at one time used a racquet seemingly wired for radar to zero in on the ball. He refused to explain his unique weapon, joking that the loops of wire set up an electromagnetic field that—like a magnet and metal— attracted the rubber of the racquetball. Other equipment notes: the minitowel tucked into his gym shorts and the lensless frames for eyeguards. (Brundage)

2
Equipment

Equipment for racquetball is minimal compared to many sports, especially if you take the gladiatorial-garb rather than the dress-to-impress approach. Whatever your taste, this guide will enable you to play safely and to hit the ball as well as your strokes allow. This chapter covers these equipment topics: (1) shoes, (2) warm-up suits, (3) brassieres, (4) eyeguards, (5) gloves and related grip slip-stoppers, (6) racquets, and (7) balls.

APPAREL

Shoes

Racquetball footwear should be heavy-duty tennis shoes or racquetball shoes. Ask a shoe dealer or pro shop salesman to recommend a good basketball shoe, since both sports involve similar quick pivoting and pushing off. If you have a history of ankle problems—sprains or strains—go with a pair of high tops for more support. Jogging shoes are impractical and unsafe for racquetball because they provide little lateral support.

Other than footwear, it is not overly important which apparel you pick along the lines of socks, shorts, and shirts. There are three important exceptions: warm-up suits, brassieres, and eyeguards.

Warm-up Suits

These are nice for warming up before a match and for cooling down afterward. A cold body that stretches violently during early play, or a hot body that suddenly cools after play, may develop cramps or muscle pulls.

Brassieres

Bras are recommended by authorities for all medium- to large-busted players. Even smaller-chested women should consider wearing a bra during racquetball games for two reasons. First, the game involves a lot of bouncing on the feet, which can cause the breasts to sag over a period of time. Second, there is real danger of injury to a breast from a direct blow by a ball or racquet. This may cause anything from a slight bruise to a hematoma (pocket of blood from a bad bruise), *but not cancer*.

Whether or not you now wear a regular bra on the court, you should consider investing in a sports bra. These provide more support, are more absorbent, the shoulder straps won't slip, and the hems and fasteners are well padded to prevent rubbing and irritation.

Eyeguards

These are a must because the ball travels faster than the eyelid can blink in racquetball. Most serious injuries in racquetball occur to the unprotected eye, and this is likely to happen to you, especially if you are a beginner or an intermediate player. At these levels, most players are usually unaware of where the ball is going and of the location of their opponent's wildly flailing racquet. Open and tournament players should also wear eyeguards. About one out of every five professional players has suffered an eye injury that has resulted in the temporary loss of vision in one eye. Eyeguards are mandatory in all Canadian Racquetball

Association (CRA) tournaments, as well as at many court clubs in the United States.

Many players who wear prescription glasses wonder if these are suitable for racquetball. They are, but only if the frames are plastic rather than metal, and if the lenses are plastic rather than glass. Note that shatterproof glass lenses may still shatter and splinter from a

Headbands are stylish and/or functional. Use one if errant strands of hair get into your eyes. Tuck the ponytail *under* the headband to avoid whiplash on the follow-through. (Stepp)

Eyeguards.

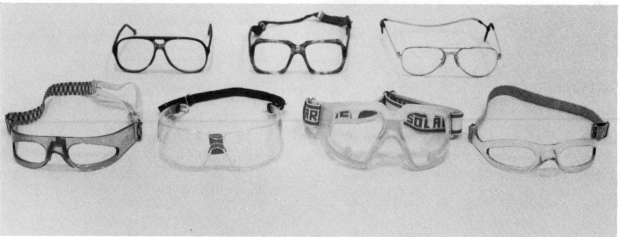

direct blow by a racquetball moving at 100 miles per hour. Tell your ophthalmologist that you want to wear your prescription glasses for protection on the court, and he or she will make sure the frames and lenses are appropriate.

A few final notes on glasses: If they slip down your nose during play, get an elastic band that hooks on to each earpiece and goes around the head. Fogging of the lenses can be prevented by using any of a number of commercial "defoggers." Finally, contact lenses (hard or soft) do not provide eye protection. Cover them with eyeguards.

COURT HARDWARE

The remainder of this chapter deals with court hardware—those items that enable you to hit the ball with your maximum potential power and accuracy. These include (1) gloves and other defenses against racquet slippage, (2) racquets, and (3) balls. First, we'll look at the defenses against grip slippage: wrist bands, gloves, and minitowels.

Wrist Bands

These are useful if the slip-causing sweat gets to your palm by running down the arm. They dam the sweat quite well, and when the bands become saturated, they should be changed. You might also look into the wrist band–thong combination unit. This device is an absorbent wrist band with a Velcro fastener, to which the racquet thong is permanently attached. This unit precludes having to make sure the thong is twisted snugly to the wrist; it also prevents the problem of the thong hooking and loosening the Velcro fasteners of your racquetball glove.

Gloves

Racquetball gloves provide perhaps the most effective means of combatting grip slippage. These, to some players, also offer a psychological boost akin to that provided to Wonder Woman when she slipped into her uniform. Choose either the full-fingered or the half-fingered glove. The latter exposes your fingers, starting at the middle knuckle joint. Some players prefer this style, claiming a superior "feel" for the racquet handle. Any glove should be

The oldest of all sweat stoppers is the wrist band, which dams the sweat that runs down your arm. Remember to put on a fresh one when yours becomes saturated, and try two wrist bands if you're an all-star sweater. In addition, realize that some bands are more absorbent than others.

The innovative wrist band–thong combination unit features an absorbent wrist band with a Velcro fastener, to which the racquet thong is attached permanently. This way, you are never without a wrist band.

thin and fit tightly, almost as a second skin. There are many glove materials from which to choose, and you should experiment to suit yourself. Gloves are usually sized from extra-small through extra-large. Most pro shops expect you to try on a potential purchase for size, and you should do so if this is your first glove or if you

Racquetball gloves.

are considering a new brand. Most gloves are washable in warm water, but you should first inspect the cleaning instructions for each particular type. Gloves do wear out eventually, and consequently they themselves can be the cause of racquet slippage. Toss them out when the palm wears so thin or gets so crusty or slick that washing doesn't help.

Minitowels

The alternative to wrist bands and gloves is the minitowel. This is a washcloth-sized piece of material that tucks into the shorts. It is used to wipe off the gloveless hand and/or racquet handle when either gets sweaty. You may purchase a minitowel, though construction is simple enough. Just cut an absorbent towel into approximately six-by-twelve-inch strips and then hem the rough edges if you wish to prevent fraying. Tuck one edge of the minitowel into your gym shorts at the right hip (assuming you are right-handed), and you're ready to wipe. When your hand or handle gets wet, lay the racquet handle onto the flappy part of the material, wrap a turn and twist with your gun hand. The towel simultaneously dries your grip as well as the racquet's grip, and it takes only a couple of seconds.

Racquets

Your racquetball racquet is the vanguard of your equipment arsenal, and as such it deserves detailed attention. Let's break the racquet into its common-feature categories and consider each individually. The feature categories include (1) frame, (2) length, (3) weight, (4) head shape, (5) grip, and (6) strings.

The most common *frame* materials are fiberglass (plastic), metal (aluminum), graphite, and wood.

The two most popular types of frame materials are fiberglass and metal. Fiberglass (plastic) racquets traditionally flex more. This means that theoretically they provide more power, owing to a greater recoil of the frame following the big flex, or give, of the frame upon ball contact. The relationship between control and flexibility is less clear-cut, though most pro players feel that the more the frame flexes, the longer the ball stays on the racquet face—thus giving more control. In all fairness to the metal

The minitowel.

The anatomy of the racquetball racquet. In addition, metal racquets frequently have rubber/plastic bumpers on the rim of the head to protect both the frame and the court walls, and to add racquet head weight.

racquet manufacturers, it should be pointed out that some of the recent aluminum frames are extruded so as to provide equivalent flexibility to fiberglass. Experiment with both materials to determine which has flexibility characteristics more compatible with your stroke and game style.

The problem with fiberglass racquets is that they may break when you accidentally hit the wall. Novice players, who during the early stages of their court careers clobber the side-walls nearly as often as the balls, should take this point to heart.

Metal racquets, on the other hand, usually are stiffer (except, as noted, for some of the newer extruded frames). Be aware that stiffness is not necessarily a detriment in stroke production, and some players prefer the inherent stiffness of metal. The big plus for metal is its durability. Most of these racquets are tough to bend and even tougher to break.

The two other frame materials are graphite and wood. Graphite racquets are sometimes described as *composites* or *graphite composites*, depending on the constituent materials. Graphite frames may be flexible or stiff, and light or heavy, depending on the ratio of graphite to other materials used to make the frame. Most graphites are more expensive than their frame material counterparts.

Wood frames are making a comeback, but these newcomers are far more sophisticated than the old wood clunkers, which had sundry disadvantages: they were too short and too heavy, the rims were too thick (which makes the strung surface area too small), the head shapes were too limited because of the nature of wood, and the grips were typically too large. The new wood frames are usually laminated and lighter, thus negating the disadvantages of the early wood racquets.

Most beginning players start with a metal racquet because of its durability. Then, as their skill improves, many opt for the fiberglass for more flexibility. Graphite and wood are no better or worse as frame materials—they simply play differently.

Racquet length is more easily chosen than frame material by the racquet buyer. Two different length racquets are marketed today: the

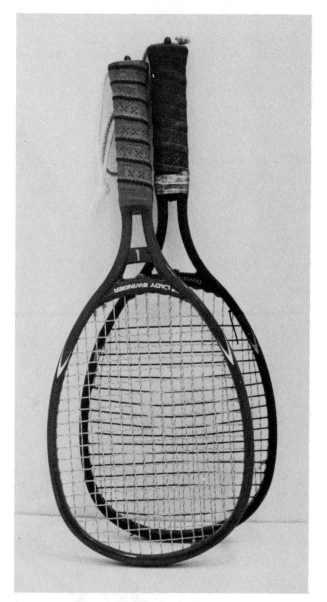

The two most common length racquets marketed today are the standard (left) and the extralong (right).

standard and the extralong models. The latter is about an inch longer and therefore offers a little more reach, a little more leverage, and a little more weight. These factors may not be beneficial for modern racquetball, in which the name of the game is power and fast reaction. The standard can be brought around on the swing faster than the extralong, which means more power, and less time required to set up on each shot. Only about one out of eight pros uses the extralong, though you should experiment with each before making a final decision on racquet length.

Racquet weight is another important determinant in selecting a racquet. The evolution of the racquetball from slow to faster has precipitated a power stroke that is characterized by a very quick swing, that is, fast head speed. A lighter racquet is obviously better suited for swinging more quickly. Still, remember that this is somewhat of a trade-off in that though you increase stroke head speed with a lighter racquet, you sacrifice the added weight behind the stroke provided by a heavier racquet.

Most racquets weigh in at 230–290 grams. A light racquet may be considered to weigh less than 240 grams, a heavy racquet above 280 grams. Again, personal preference is the determining factor here, and experimentation is the only way to discover which weight feels most comfortable to you.

Head shape is a relatively minor concern compared to the other factors involved in choosing a racquet. There are three basic head shapes: the tear drop, the rectangular (quadriform), and the round. Each offers different playing features, but none is superior to the others.

A more pertinent point of consideration along these lines is the bumper, which fits on a groove on the top of the racquet head. The bumper not only protects the racquet frame, but it also adds head weight. Thus, it greatly affects a racquet's balance. (The balance is a somewhat arbitrary term defined here as the ratio of the handle weight to the head weight. Hence, racquets are often labeled head-light or head-heavy.) Be aware that if you remove the bumper from a normally bumpered racquet, it becomes too head-light and the racquet handle may slip in your hand upon ball contact. It is more reasonable to lighten a racquet by removing the bumper, cutting off an inch or so, and replacing it in its rim groove. If you try this, a dip into hot water makes the removed rubber-plastic bumper more pliable for easier replacement.

The line-up. These four racquets portray the different head shapes. From left to right: oval head, rectangular (quadrangular) head, and teardrop head. The racquet on the right is the antiquated wooden clunker.

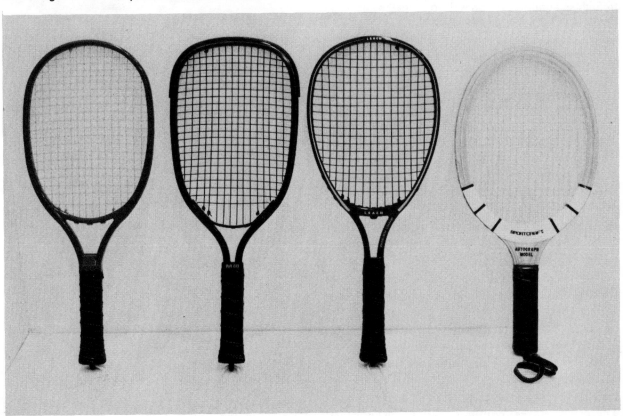

Your racquet is the most important piece of equipment from the standpoint of how well you'll hit the ball. Note the different grips and head shapes.

Grip material and *size* are the next questions. The material options usually include leather and rubber. Leather grips wear longer and are easier to regrip. However, do not be deluded that just because a leather grip has not worn out to the point of having a hole, it will not wear out. They do wear, but in a different manner—by getting slimy or slick. This can at first be cured with a warm water bath, but sooner or later the grip will become slick beyond help, and you should regrip. Most players who use leather grips also wear gloves, since leather is slippery when wet.

Rubber grips are less expensive per unit than leather, though this economy is negligible since rubber wears out faster. Rubber grips erode especially fast when there is the added friction of a glove against the grip. Players who use rubber grips find the minitowel useful to sop up handle sweat.

Grip size is just as important as grip material. There are three common sizing systems for

The two most common types of grip material are leather (left) and rubber (right).

racquet handles: (1) The "word" system labels grips extra-small through extra-large. Most male players use a medium or larger, whereas most women use a small or smaller. (2) The "inches" system gives an exact measurement of handle circumference. The normal range is from about 3⅝ inches to 4⅝ inches with ⅛-inch or 1/16-inch increments available. Most men use a 4⅛-inch grip or larger, and most women a 4-inch grip or smaller. (3) The "two-size" system is utilized by the major racquet company to facilitate manufacturing and consumer selection. The two sizes include the standard and the small. About ninety percent of male players require the standard, and ninety percent of female players the small.

There are two important additional points on grip size. The first concerns the fallacy that the racquet grip should be of similar circumference to the tennis grip. This is wrong; you should actually experiment with a smaller grip size. Racquetball uses a much more wrist-oriented stroke with its shorter racquet, and you'll find that a smaller grip lends itself better to this. The second point on grip size is that handles may be customized regarding circumference. This is a matter of removing the leather or rubber grip and shrinking or building up the handle. Shrinking works only on wood handles. Here you file the handle down evenly to the desired size, then replace the grip. Building works equally well on any handle material: You wrap a few layers of tape around the handle to increase its thickness, then replace the grip.

Strings are the final feature category for racquet selection. This subject includes string material and string tension. String material is of little concern to the beginning to intermediate player. Racquetball racquets are almost universally strung with nylon—either monofilament (tournament) nylon or multifilament nylon. Cheap racquets often use a cheap grade of nylon, better racquets a higher-quality nylon.

String tension provides a much more lively topic for discussions in club locker rooms and jacuzzis. Most racquets are factory strung at twenty-eight to thirty-two pounds of tension, which should be fine for the vast majority of players. However, court experience breeds a certain fickleness regarding string tension. The

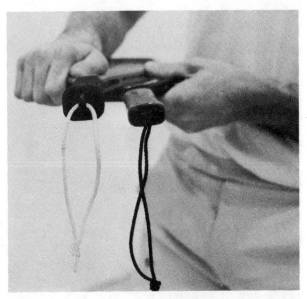

Grip size and grip shape should not be confused. There are three common sizing systems, all based on handle circumference: word system, inches system, and two-size system. On the other hand, grip shape refers to the shape of the handle, which is best seen by viewing the butt end of the racquet. The handle on the left is more rounded and the one on the right, sometimes termed the ping-pong grip, is more rectangular. Experiment with various handle sizes, as well as with different shapes.

gist of this is theoretical but logical: A looser tension gives greater power, and possibly more control, on the stroke. The rationalization here is that the strings "give" more upon ball contact with a looser tension, and consequently they recoil more for enhanced power. Similarly, the racquetball stays on the string longer with a looser tension, thereby providing increased control. The advanced player often experiments with varying string tensions—within a range of about twenty-two to thirty-two pounds. A tension below about twenty-two pounds may give the *butterfly net effect*, in which the racquet almost catches the ball instead of hitting it. A tension above about thirty-two pounds may cause the *board effect*, in which the racquet feels as stiff as a board upon ball contact.

Note that whatever the original tension, your racquet will lose two to four pounds during the first week of play as the strings stretch and "seat" in the frame. Do not worry about this since nothing can be done about it anyway.

Another related matter to which you will eventually have to acquiesce concerns broken strings. Even high-quality nylon breaks sooner

The racquetball—you serve it, slice it, kill it, and sometimes even talk to it. Karin Walton cajoles the ball before serving to Marriott. It must work—she won this match en route to the 1979 professional championship. (Charfauros)

or later, the frequency of breakage depending on the amount of play. (The one exception is the racquet whose strings break repeatedly in a certain area. This is diagnostic of a broken or missing grommet—the plastic or metal cylinder through which the string passes within the frame.) You may get just a one-string patch job, though this gives different playability on different areas of the strung surface. It makes more sense to have an entire restringing job done, either by sending the racquet to the manufacturer or by digging up a competent restringer. Whichever you choose, be sure to specify the type of string and tension desired. Also, tape your name and phone number to the handle in case the racquet is misplaced.

Besides examining the important feature categories when choosing a racquet—frame, length, weight, head shape, and strings—there are a few other minor considerations. Autographs on racquets (autograph models) may or may not be an indication of quality. Base your selection more on how you feel about the racquet itself. Racquet covers are another extra often used to lure prospective customers. Covers are unnecessary (nylon string is water resistant and most frames are noncorrosive) unless you plan to sandwich your racquet between sweaty gym clothes in your gym bag. The price tag on a racquet is not a precise indicator of quality. A medium-priced racquet often hits better than a more expensive one, though you should suspect any very cheap racquet. Finally, check out the warranty card that comes with most racquets. This usually guarantees the frame against any breakage except misuse, and the length of warranty depends on the frame material. Typically, fiberglass frames are guaranteed for about three months and metal for a year; the warranty period for graphite and modern wood varies.

Racquet selection should now pose few problems. This especially will be true if, before you

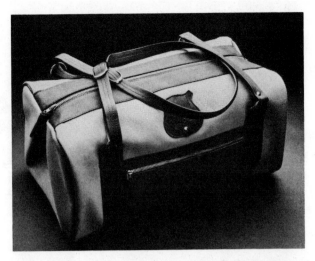

Racquetball bags have evolved from plastic sacks and paper bags to the sophisticated carrier pictured here. Many modernday bags feature a separate pocket for your racquet and another plastic-lined pocket for soiled gym clothes. Actually, anything can be used to tote court gear. (Ektelon and Phillips Org.)

shell out any money, you borrow and try out the same model that you plan to buy. It often takes only a dozen hits to differentiate a lemon from a winner.

The *racquetball* is the last piece of court equipment in this section. The selection of a good ball, once a simple chore of buying the sole ball manufactured, is now a mind-boggling task due to the vast array available. Let's simplify matters by stating that a ball is either fast or slow, and a ball is either pressurized or nonpressurized (pressureless). A slower, nonpressurized ball is best for beginning to intermediate players. The slow (less bounce) characteristic allows the novice more time to chase down and set up on each shot. This leads to the quicker development of proper strokes and of court positioning. The nonpressurized characteristic is important because these balls are generally much more durable and more consistent than their pressurized kinfolk. Increased durability means you spend less money replacing broken balls, while increased consistency means you don't have to worry about out-of-round balls.

Pro player Sarah Green. (Leach)

3
Coordination Drills and Warm-ups

You need this chapter, and you may need it badly because there are three killers on the court. The first is spasticity, the second is injury, and the third is fatigue/muscle weakness. These killers can get you—cause you to lose matches, or worse—no matter how perfect your strokes or how logical your strategy. I'm not pronouncing you doomed to be a tired, injured spastic before you even have a chance to win your first club championship. No, you can beat the three court killers with a little preparatory training before you step onto the court. This chapter tells you how.

Information on the following pages is divided into three sections, each of which reveals how to conquer one of the three aforementioned killers. The first section covers coordination drills, whose goal is to transform you from spastic klutz into graceful athlete. The second section discusses stretches, through which we'll pick off the deadly assassins of injury—pulls, strains, and sprains—before they have a chance to pick you off. The third section is devoted to warm-ups, which will give you the strength and endurance to run around the court for a full three-game match.

I don't claim that this chapter is a complete guide to coordination, stretching, and warm-ups. There are probably a dozen stretches for each of the 600-plus muscles in your body, but I'll provide only a couple of representatives for each muscle group. And, there is a veritable library of books devoted specifically to strength and conditioning, so I suggest you look into these if you're an off-the-court exercise freak.

Each of the three sections in this chapter

consists of an introduction followed by the exercises themselves. The learning is easy, so let's get on with the fun of stopping the three court killers dead in their tracks.

INTRODUCTION TO COORDINATION DRILLS

"Get coordinated!" That's what I would tell most of my students if I had the heart to be so blunt. "But how?" would be their likely response, if they were objective enough to admit to being uncoordinated. No problem. This section teaches them and you how to become coordinated.

The typical female racquetball newcomer has had little sports experience. She therefore hasn't conditioned her muscles, nervous system, and eyeballs to work together in an athletic manner. Like an excited puppy in a big new yard, she is eager to explore each corner of the court but can't quite coordinate her untrained body with her unbounded zeal. She ends up running in all directions at once with tennis shoes smoking, only to have the racquetball glance unexpectedly off a sidewall and rap her on the noggin. That's okay. It hurts only the ego and it should awaken the beginner to two facts of court life.

Marci Greer takes to the air to avoid a racquetball enema. (Charfauros)

In this photo, Keeley does a cartwheel in a futile attempt to reach a pass shot, while his opponent seemingly bows in respect for the good effort. (Yost)

First, realize that you *are* in for some early ego bruises if you have only recently taken up the game. Oh, you'll be hitting serves and strokes on your first racquetball outing, just as all the instructional books preach. But I guarantee it will take at least half a dozen times out before you learn to cope with the lively bounce of the ball, the rather fiendish way it caroms off the sidewalls, and how it hides in the back corners as though it had a mind if its own within that rubber skull. Second, realize that any spasticity you display the first few times you play is only temporary.

I believe that almost all stroke and shot woes of beginning players come not from incorrect swings, but from lack of coordination. Your coordination, or lack thereof, can be traced back to genetic and inexperience causes. In racquetball, I'd say that only about 10 percent of your problems with coordination is due to inheritance from your graceless parents. The remaining 90 percent is due to inexperience, specifically in not being familiar with how the ball bounces in the court, and in lack of exposure to athletic footwork. This 90/10 ratio is actually a real advantage. The way I see it, a little practice on the drills in this section will enable you to become 90 percent coordinated, whatever your genealogy.

So, use this section to learn the bounce of the ball and the bounce of your feet on the court. In fact, consider the routines in this chapter a self-analytical quiz to determine if you are really ready to hit the hardwood with racquet in fist. If you flunk the first time through, no big deal. Just practice the drills until you become coordinated.

Hand Dribble. Stand stationary on the court, or anywhere that there is a smooth, hard floor. Dribble the racquetball with your racquet hand, as a basketball player dribbles a basketball.

See how many times you can dribble without moving your feet. Try dribbling so that the ball always peaks at about waist height. Then try dribbling with a constant chest height peak. Then at knee height.

Racquet Dribble. This is the same as the preceding hand dribble drill, only now you use your racquet to dribble the racquetball. Again, try to dribble in nearly the same spot on the floor every time so that you don't have to move your feet.

If you find this drill more difficult than the previous hand dribble, it only means that you have less racquet-to-eye coordination than hand-to-eye coordination. You'll develop more racquet control with time and practice, until this routine is a piece of cake.

As before, you can set records for maximum bounces without moving your feet at the various peaks: waist height, chest height, and knee height.

Cross-dribble. I am using a basketball in this photo sequence only to demonstrate that any ball on any flat, hard surface will do. You will probably find a racquetball on a court more handy.

This is another hand-to-eye coordination drill in which your feet remain stationary. Simply dribble the ball as before, only now alternate hands with each bounce of the ball. You are, in essence, bounce-passing the ball from one hand to the other.

How many times can you dribble at the different waist, chest, and knee heights without error?

Walking Dribble. This drill combines walking (or jogging) with dribbling. It is exactly like dribbling down a basketball court toward the basket. You'll probably use a racquetball on a racquetball court to dribble from the back wall to the front wall, then turn around (while dribbling) and dribble back to the rear wall.

Try dribbling with ball peaks at waist, chest, and knee heights. Dribble while moving forward, then backward, and then laterally. How many lengths of the court can you go without misdribbling, or going nuts?

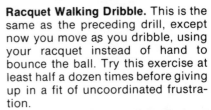

Racquet Walking Dribble. This is the same as the preceding drill, except now you move as you dribble, using your racquet instead of hand to bounce the ball. Try this exercise at least half a dozen times before giving up in a fit of uncoordinated frustration.

Go from the back wall to the front wall, then back again. Try zigzagging your way on the court. Can you run-dribble backward? Laterally? See if it is easier to dribble at waist, chest, or knee height.

Forehand Trampoline. The ball is a rubber gymnast and your racquet is a strung trampoline. The rubber gymnast bounces and bounces on the strung trampoline while you get coordinated. Actually, this drill is just an upside-down dribble.

Try to keep your feet stationary while doing this trampoline exercise, moving only when your ball angles too much to one side. Bounce the racquetball at various heights: one-foot peaks, two feet, and higher. The ceiling is the limit.

Backhand Trampoline. This is the same as the preceding drill, only now you use the flip side of the racquet to bounce the ball. You may find this backhand exercise slightly more difficult than the forehand. As before, try different heights of bounce peaks.

Do you really want a challenge? Try a running trampoline—forehand, then backhand—in which you walk (or jog) along as you simultaneously bounce the ball.

Turnover Trampoline. This is a combination of the forehand and the backhand trampoline drills. Start by bouncing the ball with your forehand. Flip the racquet over after you tap the ball so that the opposite strung face (backhand) is up. Tap the ball with your backhand. Continue alternating forehands and backhands with each ball bounce.

Is it easier to do the turnover trampoline when you bounce the ball higher or lower? Can you do this drill while moving on the court—forward, backward, laterally?

Wall Hand Dribble. This drill is a catch-and-throw sequence, but when done quickly enough it appears to be a dribble off the wall. Stand about four feet from one of the court walls. Toss the racquetball with your racquet hand at the wall just above head height. Catch the rebound with the same hand. Repeat and repeat, going faster and faster as you pick up the rhythm. How many can you do without error?

As usual, there is plenty of room for innovation on this drill. Try tossing and catching at various altitudes—from way above your head to down at your chest. Try using an underhanded toss and underhanded catch at the lower altitudes—waist- to knee-high. What happens when you move closer to the wall? Farther away? Try moving laterally along the wall while dribbling.

Wall Racquet Dribble. Use your racquet instead of your hand to dribble the ball against the wall—just the forehand for now. You may have to move your feet if your dribbles go astray.

Now do the wall racquet dribble with your backhand. This will probably be tougher than before, at least at first. Compare your average number of dribbles, maximum records, etc., using your forehand versus using your backhand.

Don't worry about the height of your racquet hits or wall hits on this drill. Just try to keep the ball in play. However, you can vary the distance of your position from the wall. You can even move closer and farther away while dribbling. Or you can try moving laterally along the wall while dribbling.

Wall Racquet Cross-dribble. This drill combines the forehand and the backhand wall racquet dribbles. Alternate hitting forehands and backhands into the wall. This means that you must angle your forehand taps a little to your left; angle your backhand taps a little to your right. If you have to hit a couple of forehands (or backhands) in a row to keep the ball in play, do so. It is more important to keep dribbling than to alternate strokes with every single swing.

What happens when you stand closer to or farther from the wall? Try the moving dribbles, too, both the farther-closer movement and the lateral movement along the wall.

Corner Hand Dribble. Stand in one of the court corners about four feet from either wall. If you choose the left rear corner, you will be about four feet from the back wall and four feet from the left side wall. Hold the ball in your racquet hand ready to toss. Now toss the ball into the left sidewall, aiming for a spot about seven feet up and about a foot from the crack juncture of the two walls. The ball will hit the left side wall, glance onto the back wall, and rebound back at your left hand in the air. Catch it with that hand. That's one lap. Now hand the ball back to your right hand and do some more laps.

The corner hand dribble may give newcomers fits because two wall rebounds are involved. That's the idea! This drill gets you accustomed to the bounce of the ball as it angles out of the rear court corners. Try moving more than four feet from the corner for this drill. Try tosses that are higher, lower, softer, harder. Can you throw with your left hand and catch with your right? Throw with your right hand and catch with your right? Try a floor bounce before catching. Try anything.

Corner Racquet Dribble. Now dribble in the corner with your racquet instead of your hand. The only difference between this and the preceding drill is your court position. Start the exercise by standing about six feet from either wall in one of the court corners. This increased distance gives you a little more reaction time to compensate for the faster ball velocity provided by the racquet.

Let's assume you start in the left rear corner of the court again. Tap the ball with your forehand into the left side wall, then catch it with your left hand following the second (back) wall rebound. Repeat. How close can you get to the corner and still maintain the dribble? How far away?

Overhand Throw. Throwing the ball with an overhand motion is very similar to hitting a forehand ceiling ball in racquetball. In fact, when you start hitting forehand ceiling shots, it might help to pretend you are throwing the ball toward the ceiling with your racquet.

Take a starting stance on the court near the back wall with the racquetball in hand. Note: Ladies frequently have trouble with this and with the next throwing drill because they hold the ball incorrectly. They grasp it fully against their palm as if cradling an apple

(caption continued on next page)

about to be eaten. Wrong! Instead, hold the racquetball for throwing as the first photo in this sequence shows—using your fingers and thumb rather than your palm to support the ball.

Now take a good windup for the overhand throw, starting with most of your body weight on your rear foot at the top of the windup. Step forward with your lead foot and throw the ball at the front wall. Aim about head-high and so that the ball rebounds directly back to you after a single floor bounce. Catch, then repeat.

Your first few throws should be warm-up tosses to limber up your throwing arm. So, toss change-ups instead of fastballs initially. Then, after your arm is loosened up with a few soft tosses, throw some moderate fastballs. Experiment. What happens when you take a deeper or a higher windup? When you rotate your body more on the windup? When you take a longer stride forward with the lead foot? When you release the ball from your hand a little earlier? A little later?

Sidearm Throw. This is the same as the previous drill, with one significant exception. Now you are going to throw the ball with a sidearm rather than an overhand. The sidearm motion is remarkably similar to the forehand kill shot stroke. There are equivalent backswings, wrist cocks, body rotations on the windup, weight transfers, steps forward with the lead foot, ball releases, and follow-throughs. Study this drill photo sequence to pick out these components of the sidearm throw. Compare this sequence to those of the forehand stroke in chapters 5 and 10.

The starting stance for the sidearm throw is again near the back wall. Be sure to hold the ball with your fingers and thumb, rather than cradling it against your palm. Throw and catch, throw and catch—until the motion becomes smooth and unconscious. As before,

the first few tosses should be softer warm-ups, then throw harder. Strive for a proper mix of maximum power with maximum accuracy.

You will discover new ways of throwing only when you experiment. Try out the variations I mentioned at the end of the preceding drill. There are also other areas to experiment in. What happens when you cock your wrist a little more for the throw? When you raise your elbow a little higher on the windup? When you rotate your shoulders a little more toward the right rear corner on the windup? Rotate your hips a little more? When you step a little more toward the left front corner with your stride into the throw? More toward the right front corner? When you throw slightly more underhanded? Slightly more overhanded?

The jerk stretch, which is the traditional vigorous bounce stretch, may be dangerous. It is better to use the static stretch method before exercise so that you lessen the chance of injury when forced to jerk your body around on the court. (Zeitman)

INTRODUCTION TO STRETCHES

Flexibility is one of the most important factors in athletics, yet it may be the most neglected and misrepresented area. In this section I hope to convince you to start a pregame stretching program and to stretch correctly.

There are many advantages to stretching before exercising. The number one advantage lies in preventing injury. Stretching allows a greater range of movement by the muscles and joints. This means that when you reach way up to hit your first ceiling ball of a match, you won't strain the joints and musculature of your gun arm. The number two advantage is increased flexibility. Stretching provides a greater freedom of movement. To me, this means I can step and reach inches farther on each shot of a rally.

The third advantage is subtler. The flexible racquetball player has more body awareness. She has a better feel for the condition of her body and is naturally trained to detect slight upsets in her musculoskeletal system, such as the beginning of a pull or strain.

The only thing that could be called a disadvantage of stretching is that it takes a little time. But don't you think that a few minutes is a small sacrifice for all the advantages I listed? I strongly suggest you arrive at the court club early enough to allow ten minutes specifically for stretching. (In the next section you'll find that you'll need another ten minutes after stretching for the warm-ups. That's a total of only twenty minutes.) Most stretching nuts such as myself also take a few minutes after playing to stretch. This postgame limbering is especially beneficial if certain areas of your body feel tight following a tough workout.

There are two methods of stretching: the static stretch and the jerk stretch. The static stretch is more effective and safe because it lets you control the momentum of your stretch. This virtually eliminates the possibility of over-stretching a muscle or joint. In the static stretch you slowly assume the stretch position. That is, you gradually increase the intensity of the tension or pull on the area being stretched, and you hold the stretch for at least twenty seconds. No bouncing or vigorous jerks are allowed. Let me illustrate the static stretch with the familiar toe touch exercise. Bend over at the waist and reach for your toes until you start to feel just a slight pull in the back of your legs. Hold that for about five seconds, then reach down a couple of

inches farther until you again feel a slightly increased pull behind your legs. Continue these stretch-and-hold increments until you reach a maximum comfortable stretch. You might feel some mild discomfort as you stretch, but there should definitely never be any sharp pain or pull.

I call the second type of stretching the jerk stretch, though stretch gurus often term it the ballistic stretch. This is the traditional vigorous bounce stretch. The severe bounce movements in this type of stretching must not be more than the particular body part can tolerate, or you'll get muscle tears and pulls. I don't use the jerk stretch, nor do I advise you to use it.

Stretch in a warm area, preferably on a soft carpet. Do it before you warm up and after you play, if you wish. Stretch statically (gradually), holding each stretch for at least twenty seconds. Okay, now let's limber up.

Trunk Twist. Raise both arms straight up as if you were just told to reach for the sky, then clasp your hands together above your head. Now swivel your upper body in a circle while bending forward and down, to the right, backward, to the left, and around and around in slow circles.

The emphasis in this drill is not speed, but flexibility. Be aware of which body part is stretching—where and how much—as you rotate. Do ten revolutions in one direction, then reverse directions for ten more.

Single-arm Helicopter. Pretend your right arm is a helicopter blade and rotate it slowly around and around, using the shoulder as a pivot point. Again, begin slowly and then increase the speed of the exercise only after your arm has loosened up. Perform at least twenty forward revolutions, then reverse directions and rotate your arm as though throwing continuous underhanded softball pitches.

Now give your right arm a rest and do the helicopter with your left. Perform at least twenty forward and twenty reverse revolutions.

Double-arm Helicopter. This is the same as the preceding routine, only now you rotate both arms simultaneously in a forward direction. Do twenty or so revolutions, then crank it into reverse for twenty more.

An interesting variation of this exercise is rotating the arms simultaneously but in opposite directions.

Handcuff Stretch. Extend both arms behind your back somewhat like the last time you had on handcuffs, then clasp your fingers as though praying upside down. Now bend forward at the waist until you feel a slight pull or stretch in your lower back and the backs of your legs.

Hold this mild stretch position at least five seconds, then bend over a tad more. In this and in all stretches you should feel only a slight to moderate pull on your muscles, never great discomfort. Hold this increased stretch at least another fifteen seconds.

Back bow. Now you are going to become aware of how a bow feels when the archer pulls back for a long-distance shot. The back bow stretches your arms, shoulders, and back. You'll need a stationary handhold of some kind about waist-high off the floor. A horizontal bar, sturdy doorknob, or the top of the back wall in a racquetball gallery will suffice.

Reach straight behind your back with both arms as you did in the handcuff stretch, but do not clasp your hands. Instead, grab the stationary handhold with both hands. Slowly and deliberately thrust your pelvis forward until you feel the mild stretch. Hold this for at least five seconds. Then arch your back bow a little farther and hold this increased stretch position at least fifteen seconds.

Spider. The back bow limbered you up for the spider. If you are naturally tight in the back or if your back isn't loosened up enough to get into this position without discomfort, work solely on the preceding back bow stretch and skip this one.

Get into the spider position, first by lying flat on your back. Bring your heels up to your buttocks, and place your hands flat on the floor near your ears. Now just do an upside-down push-up. (Make absolutely sure the floor isn't slick when you do this exercise.) Take it easy at first, then arch into an increased stretch. Besides stretching your back, you should feel a pull on your stomach muscles. Hold for at least twenty seconds.

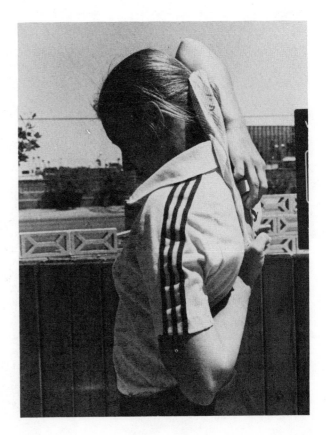

Shoulder Stretch. This one stretches your arms and shoulders. Reach around and behind your waist with your left hand, as though trying to scratch way up between your shoulder blades. That takes care of your left hand. Now reach up and over your right shoulder with your right hand until you can clasp together the ends of the fingers of both hands.

You say you can't reach that far without removing your liver? Then use a towel as an extender. Hold one end of the towel with your right hand in the shoulder stretch position, grab the other end with your left hand, and pull. Hold for at least five seconds. Work your hands closer together from either end of the towel and hold this increased stretch an additional fifteen seconds.

Now reverse arm positions, with your right hand reaching around and behind your waist and with your left hand reaching up and over your left shoulder.

Toe Toucher. This is the venerable veteran of stretches. Remember in this and in all stretches that the pull on the muscles is static and gradual rather than a jerky bounce. This stretch focuses on your hamstrings (the backs of your upper leg muscles) and your calves.

Bend forward at the waist until you feel a slight pull in the backs of your legs. Hold there for about five seconds, then reach farther down toward the ground with your hands until you feel an increased stretch. Hold for the final minimum fifteen seconds. Remember to evaluate your stretch position by the amount of pull you feel in your hamstrings and calves, not by the distance that you reach down with your hands. This stretch is called the toe toucher only in deference to tradition. Your maximum stretch might be to your knees, your sock tops, your toes, or farther.

Hamstring Stretch. This is another hamstring tugger that, if performed correctly, also stretches the sides of your upper torso. You'll need a waist- to chest-high support for your leg, such as a fence, the back of a chair, a horizontal bar, or a friendly shoulder.

Place your right heel on the support. Bend forward and sideways so that your right ear approaches your right knee. Reach your left arm up and over your head until you can grasp the toe of your shoe. At the same time, grab your heel with your right hand. Don't worry if you can't reach your foot with your hands. Go as far as feels comfortable, and no farther. You can use a towel as an extender, looping it around your instep and grabbing either end with your hands. Hold the mild stretch for at least five seconds, then stretch a bit farther for fifteen more seconds.

Now switch legs, placing your left heel on the support. Stretch your left hamstring and the right side of your upper torso.

Groin Pull. The groin pull stretches the insides of your thighs. Start by standing with your legs spread apart in a moderate split position. Lean to your left, flexing at your left knee and placing most of your body weight on your left foot. If you keep your right leg straight and in its original position, you should feel a slight pull in your right groin muscles—from your crotch down the inside of your leg to your knee. Hold five seconds, then increase the stretch and hold an additional fifteen seconds.

Now switch legs. Flex your right knee, lean right and maintain a stiff left leg. Again, hold for a total of at least twenty seconds.

Wall Push. The only prop for this calf stretcher is a solid vertical surface, such as the wall of a racquetball court. Get into a sprinter's position as though your feet were in the starting blocks at the beginning of a race to see who could crash headfirst into the wall. Start with your left foot in the rear starting block position and your right foot in the front. Lean forward until you have to brace your arms against the wall, then try to push the wall over. It probably won't give and, instead, you'll feel a stretch in the back of your left calf. Hold for five seconds, then push a little harder for at least fifteen seconds more.

Now switch legs, with the right foot in the rear starting block position. Keep the back leg that is worked in this exercise fairly straight and do not bounce. Also, keep your rear foot flat on the floor (rather than being on the ball of your foot) for a maximum calf stretch.

Sit-bend. Sit on the floor with your legs spread wide apart in front of you. Now bend at your waist to the right so that you can grab your right foot with both hands. In this position you should be listening to your right knee with your right ear. Hold for at least five seconds, then lean a little farther for fifteen seconds more.

Now repeat the stretch on your left side. The sit-bend loosens the backs and insides of your legs, plus the sides of your upper torso.

Thigh Stretch. This exercise mainly stretches your thighs. Assume the hurdler's position on the floor with your right leg extended ahead and your left leg flexed under itself (or angled slightly out to the side, if this is more comfortable). Lean forward and into your extended right leg until, as in the preceding stretch, you can touch or grab your right foot with both hands. Use a towel extender around the instep of your right foot if you have to. As before, you can listen to your knee as your right ear approaches your right leg. This pose stretches the back of your right leg and the front of your left leg. Hold for five, then fifteen, seconds.

Now reverse legs, so that you lean into your left and your right is tucked under. Do you feel a pull at the back of your left leg and the front of your right leg? Stretch statically for a minimum of twenty seconds.

Knee Licker. Sit on the floor with your legs together in front of you. Bend forward at the waist until you feel a slight pull in the backs of your legs and in your lower back. Hold the mild stretch for five seconds and the increased stretch for fifteen seconds. You may be able to grab your heels or even lick your knees. A towel extender looped around both feet may be necessary during the early workouts.

Body Ball. Start in the sit-down position as you did in the previous knee licker stretch. In this exercise, however, you roll onto your back and swing your legs over your shoulders.

There are two positions for this stretch. The first is with your legs bent so that your knees fall next to your head, as though you were trying to warm up your ears with your knees. Hold this body ball for a total of at least twenty seconds. Position two is with the legs extended straight over your head. Keep them stiff like a pair of chopsticks protruding from your gym shorts. You may grasp your toes and gently tug for additional stretch. Again, hold for a minimum of twenty seconds. These two positions stretch slightly different areas of your back and legs.

This is why it is necessary to warm up for a few minutes before any game. Forget the pregame warm-up, and you might pull a muscle while jumping and stretching for the ball during a match. Here Hogan steps into an exaggerated closed stance for a desperation forehand shot. Note the similarity between this step into the closed stance and the crossover warm-up exercise. (Leach)

INTRODUCTION TO WARM-UPS

I encourage you to spend at least ten minutes warming up before any match, whether the game is for fun or for blood and Gatorade. This warm-up is designed to get the metabolism percolating, oil the joints, alert the mind to upcoming action, and prep the muscles for overdrive. This translates into better performance on the court and a decreased incidence of injury.

The goal of this chapter is not to start a nationwide league of superwomen who are ready at the drop of a ball to leap the service box in a single bound. Rather, I want to start a movement toward warmed up bodies. Anything you do beyond that is up to you. For example, working with weights is beyond the scope of this book but not beyond the scope of feminine training. More and more female athletes are invading the male-odorous weight rooms and adding a touch of class to the stereotyped world of barbell dumbbells. I think this immigration is hunky-dory, and apparently racquetball clubs do, too, because more and more are offering weights, programs, and instructors for women.

I'll leave you to your workout with a final word of encouragement taken from my personal experience. One day when I was a high schooler who had never even heard of racquetball, I looked in the mirror and decided that my reflection was getting a little chunky. Running seemed to be the most logical solution and, being a goal getter of near-neurotic nature even in those early years, I determined to run for a full mile without stopping. I got up the first morning and made it about an eighth of a mile before my lungs got out of synch with my heart and I had to stop. The next day I was sore, so I went out and ran-walked. That is, I ran a couple of blocks, then walked a couple of blocks, ran, walked . . . until I ground out a mile. Of course, this didn't fulfill my goal of running a full mile nonstop. A full three weeks passed before I accomplished that.

You might take four lessons from this little piece of braggadocio. First, it's going to take some commitment and energy on your part.

Player-pro, Jim Schatz, serves up against racquetball guru, Carl Loveday.

Second, start slow and gradually increase the intensity of your workout. Third, even if you adhere to the previous point, you're probably going to feel sore. Don't get discouraged, and stretch out before you do tomorrow's warm-ups. Fourth, don't be surprised if, like me, you become a warm-up fanatic. Fellow author-player Victor Spear best sums up my feelings on this matter: "The day you become a bona fide racquetball player is the day you decide to get into shape to play racquetball rather than playing racquetball to get into shape."

Touch and Go. This exercise works your legs as well as your lungs. Start on the racquetball court *(below left)* with your left foot near the crack juncture of the back wall and floor. Your left hand should actually touch this crack. Push off with your left leg and sprint to the front wall *(below center)*. When you get there place your right foot near the front wall *(below right)* and bend over to touch the crack juncture with your right hand. Push off with your right leg and sprint back to the back wall *(bottom center)*. When you get there plant your left foot and touch the crack with your left hand. Push off again *(bottom right)* and continue the touch-and-go laps. Do three to ten laps, depending on your physical condition and your goals.

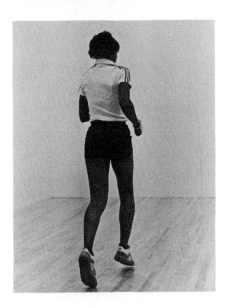

Lateral Run. This is a warm-up, a coordination drill, and a conditioner all rolled into one. Start on the court with your right foot planted on the floor near the right side wall. Push off your right leg to your left and . . .

. . . step sideways by placing your right foot behind and across your left. Then . . .

. . . bring your left foot across so that again both feet point at the front wall.

Now step sideways by placing your right foot in front of and across your left.

Move your left foot sideways so that again you are square with the front wall. Continue moving to your left with this lateral run until you reach the left side wall. Then . . .

. . . reverse directions by pushing to your right with your left leg.

Move laterally back toward the right side wall with the same four-step locomotion: left foot behind right, right foot across to square with the front wall, left foot in front of right, right foot across to square with the front wall . . .

. . . until you reach the right side wall. Now you're back in the original starting position and ready to reverse direction to run another lateral lap. Do five to twelve laps, again depending on your present condition and goals.

Crossovers. Stand on the court facing the front wall as if you were awaiting a serve—about five feet from the back wall and approximately midway between the side-walls.

Pivot on the balls of both feet so that your toes point toward the right side-wall.

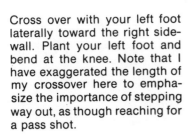

Cross over with your left foot laterally toward the right side-wall. Plant your left foot and bend at the knee. Note that I have exaggerated the length of my crossover here to emphasize the importance of stepping way out, as though reaching for a pass shot.

Now push back up off your left foot to resume the original starting position. That completes the forehand half of the crossover. Now for the backhand half . . .

. . . pivot on the balls of both feet so that your toes point toward the left sidewall.

Cross over with your right foot and plant it way out there. Again, I have exaggerated the length of my step here because crossover greenhorns invariably take too small a lateral stride. Now push back up off your right foot and . . .

. . . assume the original starting position. That completes one full crossover repetition. Go easy the first time out if your legs aren't in shape. Perform five to twelve repetitions.

Flamingo. The flamingo warm-up/coordination drill will be easy only if you have a center of gravity down around your instep. Don't get discouraged if at first you topple more than you balance. Body control comes quickly with a little practice. Start by standing on a firm surface. Raise your arms straight out at shoulder height for forthcoming balance and point your right toe to the right.

Now lift your right leg up out to the side until it is nearly parallel with the ground (or as high as you can without losing balance). Maintain this position for at least five seconds if you can. Then . . .

. . . let your leg down slowly and point the right toe forward.

Now lift your right leg up straight ahead until it is nearly parallel with the ground. Hold at least five seconds if possible, then . . .

. . . return the right foot slowly to the ground and point your toe to the rear.

Lift your right leg up and behind you until it is nearly parallel with the ground. Freeze for five seconds.

Everything up to now has made you aware of what it feels like to be a left-legged flamingo. Now go through the right-legged flamingo routine, where you lift your left leg off the ground in three separate movements: laterally, forward, and backward. Remember that you should not kick up to each position. Lift the leg slowly and then freeze at the peak height for at least five seconds.

Adler Agility Exercise. This drill is such a kick that you'll soon forget that the goals are warming up and getting coordinated. It starts innocuously enough with you just standing there ready to jump into it. Take note of this starting stance *(top left)* because you will be jumping back to it after each of a series of tricks. Ready?

Trick number one *(top center)* is simply jumping from the starting stance to a place on the ground about three feet ahead. Now jump back to the original starting position.

Trick number two *(top right)* is a jump about three feet backward. Then jump back to the original starting stance.

Trick number three *(above left)* is a jump of about three feet to your left side. Then back to the starting position.

Trick number four *(above center)* is a jump to your right about three feet away. Then back to the original starting stance.

Trick number five *(above right)* is a quarter turn to your left. You should land facing left (a ninety-degree turn). Then jump back to the original starting stance.

Trick number six is a half turn to your left. You should land facing backward relative to your takeoff stance (a 180-degree turn). Then jump back to the original starting stance.

Trick number seven is a three-quarter turn to your left. In this photo I'm still spinning and will land facing to the right relative to my takeoff position (a 270-degree turn). Then I'll jump back in the reverse direction to the original stance.

Trick number eight is a full 360-degree turn to your left. It isn't easy unless your mother was a pogo stick. You should . . .

. . . land facing forward in the original starting stance.

Trick number nine is a quarter turn (ninety degrees) to your right, then back to the starting stance. Trick number ten is a half turn to your right (180 degrees), then back. Trick number eleven is a three-quarter turn (270 degrees) to your right, then back. Trick number twelve is a full turn (360 degrees) to your right, which puts you back in the original position. Then do a 360-degree jump in the reverse direction to complete the routine.

    Perform the twelve tricks of the Adler Agility Exercise three to ten times, or until you get dizzy. Innovate. Try it slow, fast, with your feet together, feet apart. It can even be done on one leg!

Loveday Limber-ups. Introduction: The Loveday Limber-ups routine was developed by the great-grandfather of racquetball, Carl Loveday. These drills, designed to build stamina, strengthen the legs, and improve footwork, could just as easily be called an exercise in scrambled footwork.

The required equipment is a flat place to run (such as a racquetball court) and five or more "ABC Loveday" frisbees. Or you can use any old frisbees. Or folded towels, racquet covers, racquetball cans, or hats. Place the frisbees about four feet apart in a straight line. You may want to vary this frisbee-to-frisbee distance slightly according to your height.

You may begin to feel a slight pain in your legs if you do enough laps in each of the following Loveday Limber-ups. Nothing sharply uncomfortable, but a mounting sensation that your legs are getting a vigorous workout. In the exercise argot this is known as burn and it means that the exercise is doing you some good. When you start to feel the burn, finish one more lap and quit. After you have built up your stamina, it will take longer before the burn comes. Perform the Loveday Limber-ups routine no more than every other day.

Loveday Limber-up I. Start in line with the frisbees behind #1. Run to the left of #1, to your right between #1 and #2, to your left between #2 and #3, to your right between #3 and #4, and so on, until you reach the end of the row. As you circle the final frisbee, reverse directions so you now return toward the starting station while running backward. In other words, the first half of the lap is running forward and the return trip is running backward (facing the same direction throughout the lap).

Therefore, limber-up I is simply a continuous series of figure eights done at a good clip. The most important thing in this first variation of the routine is to take very *short steps* (ten to sixteen inches) while staying on your toes. Don't lift your feet too far off the floor. Limit the length of your stride, and avoid running flat-footed.

Loveday Limber-up II. This is the high-step variation of the limber-ups. That is, you trace exactly the same path as in limber-up I, but now you raise your knees very high as you zigzag through the line of frisbees. Take the same short steps and keep up on your toes—just high-step it. When you reach the last frisbee in the row, high-step it in reverse back to the start, still facing in the same direction.

The high-stepping exercise is designed to work the push-off muscles of your thighs. You will also experience a burn sensation in your calves if the exercise is done with short steps while keeping on the toes.

Loveday Limber-up III. Same starting stance behind frisbee #1. Push off your right foot and land on the left toe on the left side of the line of frisbees. Then push off the left foot and land on the right toe on the right side of the row. Then to the left side and so on until you reach the end of the line. Then return to the start by jumping from side to side while going backward—still facing the same direction as before.

We are interested in the *lateral jump* more than the forward jump in this limber-up routine. When you jump from one foot to the other (side to side), you should advance only about one-third of the distance between any two frisbees. This means a lateral leap of perhaps 4 feet combined with a forward leap of only about 1½ feet.

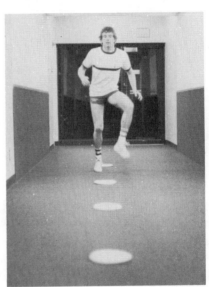

Loveday Limber-up IV. This is another high-step exercise with steps similar to limber-up II. Take short steps, land on your toes, and raise your knees. This variation is similar to the tire drill routine that football players do for agility, leg strengthening, and wind. You've probably seen those footballers high-stepping down a double row of tires, alternately placing the left foot in the left row and right foot in the right row while advancing forward. Same thing, only without the possibility of spraining an ankle on a tire with a misstep.

Take the usual starting station and start high-stepping down the line of frisbees. You should straddle the row of frisbees as you move forward to simulate stepping into tires. Keep the left foot on the left side of the row, the right foot on the right side. Keep your feet just a little wider than shoulder width—no lateral leaps as in limber-up III. Run quickly and keep your knees as high as possible without kicking yourself in the chin.

Reverse direction when you reach the end of the row, still facing the same direction. In other words, high-step in reverse back to the start. Repeat as many laps as you can before the burn sensation starts to set in. Then finish the lap, quit, rest a couple of minutes and go on to the next limber-up variation.

Loveday Limber-up V. The starting place for this limber-up variation is about two feet to the left of frisbee #1. Face that frisbee with your left side pointing down the row. Bring your right foot behind and across your left foot and put it on the floor. Then bring your left foot in front of and across your right foot and place it down. Continue to sidle sideways along the left side of the frisbee row until you reach the last frisbee. Go around this final frisbee and continue back up the right side of the row.

When you get back to frisbee #1, alter your course. Now you start down the right side of the row. That is, you begin on the right side while facing frisbee #1. Your left foot comes behind and across your right foot and plants on the floor. Then your right foot comes in front of and across your left foot and plants. Continue down the line, circle the final frisbee, and head back to frisbee #1 along the left side of the row.

The final step on the Loveday Limber-ups is yours. Invent your own variations—there must be dozens.

Chin-ups. Chin-ups, a throwback to the days when folks played in trees instead of courts, increase bicep and grip strength. You simply find a horizontal bar or limb, latch on and . . .

. . . pull up. Then let yourself down slowly—all the way down—and repeat. It is important to let yourself down slowly from the chinned position because this is the phase of negative resistance of the exercise, which builds strength as does the positive resistance phase of the actual chinning. It is also important to chin all the way up and then let yourself all the way down to the fully extended arm position to ensure a maximum range of movement. This maximum range of movement provides stretching of the muscles about to be stressed, which is desirable as explained in the introduction to stretches.

Is it easier or harder when you chin up using an overhand grip rather than the underhanded one shown here? Does it work the same muscles?

Push-ups. Push-ups are another one of the granddaddies of exercises. These are very practical when you consider that the only props required are a surface and gravity. Start down and . . .

. . . push up. Go slowly and make sure your arms fully extend in the up position. Try to keep your back fairly straight throughout and let yourself down slowly—the negative resistance phase—until your chest just touches the ground. Repeat the push-up cycle up and down, up and down.

If you don't have the upper body strength to do a regular push-up yet, start with "girls" push-ups, in which your knees partially support you by resting on the ground. You should still keep your back straight. Push-ups with a closer hand spread work the triceps more, while a wider hand spread gets the chest muscles involved. Try both.

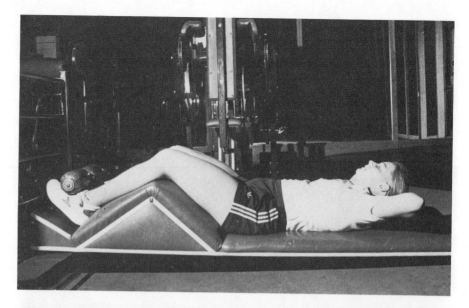

Sit-ups. Back to the basics again with gut tightening sit-ups. A padded inclined board is nice but not mandatory for this exercise. All you really need is something to hold your feet down (such as a sit-up partner). Begin by lying there feigning sleep, and then . . .

. . . sit up. Keep your hands clenched behind your head so that you can't use the momentum of your arms to bring you up. This is a stomach, not an arm, exercise. Sit up slowly and, just as important, let yourself down slowly rather than collapsing. Another significant point: the bent-knee sit-ups shown here are superior to straight-leg sit-ups because they make the stomach rather than the thigh muscles do the work. Also, slightly flexed knees put less of a strain on the lower back.

Jump Rope. Jumping rope is a good conditioner for the legs and lungs, gives you twinkle-toe footwork, and makes you feel like a kid again. The types of jumping routines are limited only by your imagination. Try jumping forward, backward, two-legged, one-legged, alternate legs, moving forward, moving backward, going in a circle, high jumps, low jumps, single jumps, double jumps.

Count jumps if you wish. Set records, keep a record, adhere to a strict routine, or just jump in synch with the cosmic pulse of the universe or you can skip to the beat of music or to the metronome of your breathing.

Jogging. Coming . . .

. . . coming . . .

. . . gone! I jog/run regularly and I admit to being a zealous proselytizer of running. It's a very cheap form of exercise, as well as a decent way to get from one place to another. I have only three admonitions: stretch your legs for five minutes before *and* after you run, invest in a quality pair of running shoes, and avoid hard surfaces such as pavement if your knees or legs are inclined to get sore.

You needn't set the track on fire if you're a newcomer to this method of locomotion. In fact, force yourself to start slow and easy the first few times out. Try to cover half a mile with a "run and walk," in which you jog until you tire, then walk until you recoup, then jog again, and so on. As you shape up, you'll feel better on and off the court. Then you can increase the length of your runs.

How much to run? That's up to you. I suggest you set a goal of time rather than distance once you've established a base of conditioning. Work your way up to twenty minutes at least three times a week. It doesn't matter how far you go as long as you're on the move for at least twenty minutes. How fast to run? Again, this is an individual matter. I don't care if you jog, slog (slow jog), or run, just as long as you get your feet moving.

Do you need further motivation? Then get a running buddy, or organize a group of joggers. Consider getting to the court early and running with your racquetball partner before playing, or staying later for a postgame run. You might want to keep track of your time or distance covered during each run with a graph chart that shows at a glance where you've been, where you are, and where you're going. The bottom line, however, is that you must motivate yourself to take the first step.

Perky Sarah Green follows through after a forehand hit. Her grip is a little higher on the handle than I recommend, and it appears she has contacted the ball a little high—at her waist—but who can argue with the technique of a fellow pro and former amateur national champ? (Leach)

4
Forehand Grip

The strokes in racquetball include the forehand and the backhand. Hit forehands on the right side of your body, backhands on the left side of your body. That doesn't leave much room for originality or innovation, though you'd swear some players refuse to acknowledge this when they scrunch their carcasses against the left sidewall when running around their feeble backhands to use a stronger forehand stroke. I suppose these players could be said to have two forehands, in the same way that some folks have two left feet.

The originality in stroke work comes not with the separation of the forehand and backhand but with the way different individuals swat the ball. For example, two-time national champ Peggy Steding strokes the ball in a radically different way from me, two-time national champ Shannon Wright. Peggy uses a short and wristy swing, where mine is more of a loop with a bullwhip crack at ball contact. Yet, judging by our court credentials, we each seem to be hitting the ball properly for our individual physiotypes and game styles.

Similarly, the correct stroke for you is probably not exactly the right one for the next player. There is no way that a 5'10", 135-pound player will—or should—swing a racquet like a 5', 95-pound player.

That there is one proper stroke, or model stroke, for all players is a fallacy perpetuated by lackadaisical instructors and by instructional texts. From a teaching instructor's viewpoint, it is decidedly easier to walk into the court and sagely announce, "Here is how I hit the ball . . . got it? That is the proper stroke. Now you do exactly the same, and I'll see you next week for the backhand lesson." This obviously is not the ideal teaching method, especially in a one-on-one instructor-student situation. On the other hand, I'll grant that in a clinic format where one pro lectures and demonstrates to a group of players, the monkey-see-monkey-do learning technique is the only practical approach. I use it because if I went one-on-one when teaching the forehand and backhand strokes to each of thirty students in a clinic, we wouldn't get past the backswing.

The other area where a singular proper, or model, stroke for all players is used is in an instructional book—such as this one. This is out of necessity, as when teaching to a clinic group. However, let me explain how I would teach you or anyone else the strokes in a private individual lesson. Unless my student has absolutely never stroked a racquetball before, I initially tell her to hit a few balls with her normal forehand (or backhand). She does, and my experienced eye usually picks out a couple of gross errors in the stroke. I point out one of these errors, tell her how to correct it and why, then have her hit a few more balls with the improved swing. Then I point out the other stroke error, tell her how to correct it and why, and have her hit away with this, the right stroke for her.

Let's illustrate this learning process with a specific example. Consider the apocryphal anecdote of Magnolia Morepower. Maggie had a sweet stroke before she came to me for tips, with two points of exception—she usually forgot to take both a backswing and a follow-through. I noticed this when she took a few practice swings for me, and I gently urged her to make one correction at a time. First I said, "Magnolia, I think you'd generate more power if you took a backswing before hitting the ball. Watch me hit one . . . just like that." So she took a backswing before hitting the ball and was pleased to find she could whack it about 20 percent harder than before. Then I announced the second correction: "Magnolia, now that you've got the backswing down, I think you'd generate more power if you followed through after striking the ball. Watch my follow-through on this stroke . . . just like that. Now you try it." You can guess that when Magnolia added a follow-through to the backswing on her stroke, she hit the ball like Marty Hogan in a tutu. Her

It is possible to use a slightly improper grip and still swat a decent smasheroo, because with practice the body makes adjustments to smooth out grip as well as stroke mistakes. The problem with adapting to slightly improper techniques is that when you are stressed by nerves or by a rushed swing, the weak link in your grip or stroke is amplified. This is because under stress the body doesn't have either the presence of mind or the time to compensate for that weak link. In this photo, does pro player Linsey Meyers have a grip on things here? If not, he'd better be holding his racquet correctly. (Brundage)

booming shots moved the front wall back with each swing.

You should have learned from this anecdote that the ideal teaching method is just the opposite of the traditional method utilized in clinics and instructional books. With Magnolia, I had her take her normal stroke and then adapted that swing to the model stroke. In this book, however, I am forced to present the model strokes and have you adapt to them and butcher them as you may.

The model stroke, by my definition, is that swing (forehand or backhand) which is the easiest and fastest to learn by the most players with the best results. The model strokes are the universal swings that, if everyone was an average player, would serve as excellent patterns for all to emulate.

With that disclaimer out of the way, let's talk briefly about feedback. You should seek outside input about your strokes. This feedback can be something as sophisticated as a videotape analysis, or something more practical like a buddy screaming in your ear, "Take a backswing, Magnolia, you clod!"

Then, after you receive intelligent and constructive criticism about your strokes, be open-minded enough not to just pooh-pooh it in rejection. This happens all the time—especially among court peers—and the player receiving the criticism doesn't benefit, while the person giving the advice certainly won't feel inclined to offer it again. I once instructed a player in California who had a strange request at our initial lesson. (This anecdote, unlike that of Magnolia Morepower, really happened.) This gal walked onto the court and the first thing she said was, "Hi. I'm happy with my strokes. I've been doing sports all my life and I'm coordinated enough to clobber the ball pretty hard. My problem is that every ball goes into the front wall three feet high. Every stupid one! I'll be satisfied with this series of lessons if only you can show me how to kill the ball low on the front wall." So I told her to drop and hit a couple of shots using her normal stroke. She obliged, and she was right. She did clobber the ball with a picturesque stroke—but it sent almost every shot into the front wall three feet high. The too-high problem was easy to diagnose because I had seen it many times before. I told her she was contacting the ball waist high, which is fine for tennis or baseball hitting but results in a "squash" (too-high) kill in racquetball. "You have to lower your point of ball contact to knee high or lower," I said.

"I *am* hitting it knee-high," she snapped, and then demonstrated by dropping and hitting the ball. Again, her contact was at waist height.

"That was waist-high," I pointed out.

"No, watch more closely," she said, and she dropped and hit the ball at her waist again. "You see?" she said. "I contact the ball at my knees and it *still* goes into the front wall three feet high. What's the problem?" The problem was that her self-image and actual swing were about two feet in disagreement. This gal just lacked a little body awareness, a frequent occurrence among beginning racquetballers. The solution to the problem?

"Please try this for me," I said. "Contact a few shots ankle-high." The gal looked at me doubtfully, then dropped and hit the ball into the front wall. The height of her ball contact on the stroke—though supposedly ankle-high—was exactly at knee height. Predictably, the ball zoomed off her strings and into the front wall only inches up from the floor. Terrific! I instructed her to hit a few more at ankle height. She did and the shots went in for nearly perfect roll-offs. Then my student, though obviously pleased with the dramatic lowering of her shots, nevertheless could not resist chiding *my* ostensible teaching ineptness. "Why didn't you tell me I had to contact the ball ankle-high in the first place?!"

The moral of the story is, "If only we could see our strokes as other people see them." Well, we can't—but we *can* solicit criticism and try out constructive suggestions. Discard the ideas that don't help you and incorporate into your strokes the ones that do.

In this and the next three chapters, trust my model grips and strokes as good guidelines to proper technique. Next, get feedback. Then, practice, practice, practice—that's what the drills in chapter 10 are for. But, like the player whose feet are quicker than the rest of her body, we're getting ahead of ourselves without even starting. Let's begin with the forehand—first the grip, then the stroke.

FOREHAND GRIP PREVIEW

I've had many students who have admirable swings, but who use an aborted grip to grasp the racquet. An improper grip usually negates the most perfect stroke, rendering it ineffective.

Let me describe a situation I've come across dozens of times in my teaching that demonstrates the importance of using a proper grip. In this common error, the gal grabs the racquet handle as though it were a Neanderthal club. Her hand wraps around the grip in a tight fist with the palm behind (this will be explained) the handle. You'd think this lady was going dinosaur hunting instead of pursuing a little ball. In fact, this mis-grip seems natural to so many court greenhorns that it may have been passed down genetically from our dinosaur-clubbing ancestors. If you give a beginning player a racquet and tell her to shake hands with it in

The improper fist grip is perhaps the most common of all forehand grip errors. The racquet is not a club. If you hold it as such, your forehand shots will likely skip into the floor.

typical grip fashion, I'll bet she shakes hands with this improper palm-behind-the-handle fist grip before the racquet has a chance to shake back and say, "pleased to meet you." The problem with this mis-grip is that it causes the racquet to angle toward the floor (closed face) when ball contact is made. This, in turn, directs the ball toward the floor for a skipped shot—again and again.

I'm not saying that you cannot hit the ball decently with a slightly improper grip or stroke. You can, because if you practice even a wrong technique long enough it becomes efficient. For example, my forehand stroke used to be far from picturebook perfect. I used to push rather than pop my forehand at ball contact. Yet, I was successful with my spastic swing because I had hit thousands of practice shots with it over a period of a year. During that practice, my body adapted to the incorrect push swing by compensating in other areas.

Indeed, *your* body is an excellent adjuster

when it comes to smoothing out grip and stroke mistakes—if these are only minor errors. And the nice thing about the body as a compensatory mechanism is that it adapts without your realization of it. Reconsider the case of the Neanderthal club grip. The body naturally adapts to this improper downward inclination of the racquet face (closed face) by having the right hitting shoulder dip and by causing the ball to be contacted farther forward than normal. The result is level shots rather than skip balls.

Your immediate question should be, "What's the use of worrying about the proper grip and stroke if the body neatly transforms it all into an effective stroke?" The problem with adapting to improper techniques surfaces in two instances: (1) when your swing is rushed on a setup that offers little setup time, or (2) when you stroke in a stressful situation, as when you're nervous at 20-20 in a big match. Either of these conditions amplifies the weak links in your stroke. The body doesn't have either the time or the presence of mind to adapt when the swing is rushed or stressed. Relating this to the closed-face Neanderthal grip, when rushed or stressed, the body isn't able to compensate for the bad grab (by dipping the right shoulder and contacting the ball farther forward). The sad result is that the ball skips into the floor on rushed or stressed swings.

This is only one example of why you should start with good solid techniques rather than force your body to accommodate faulty ones that will fall apart under pressure. Let's start now with the most basic of all racquetball techniques—the forehand grip. Get a racquet out of your gym bag—right this minute. Use it as you progress through the following steps. Otherwise, I guarantee you'll end up with an improperly rotated mind.

FOREHAND GRIP TECHNIQUE

Before we begin, I'm pleased to announce to all court newcomers that the racquetball racquet has a throat, head, face, and butt—just like the rest of us. The racquet's anatomy is somewhat misplaced, however. The head is everything above the handle, and the face is the strung hitting surface on the head. The throat, of course, is just below the face. The throat slims down into the handle, and this continues down—curiously without interruption of arms or legs—to the butt or terminal bump of the racquet's handle. (See illustration.)

1. Grasp the throat of your racquet with your nonracquet (left) hand. Hold the racquet in front of and out from your waist, so that the strung face is perpendicular to the floor.

2. Grasp the racquet handle with your hitting (right) hand as though you were shaking hands with the racquet.

3. Check to see that the palm of your hand lies in about the same perpendicular-to-the-floor plane as the face. Or, your palm should lie along and be in the same plane as the flat surface on the right side of the handle.

4. This step relates to the previous one and ensures that the racquet is properly rotated within your hand . . . or:

First, you must become familiar with the thumb-finger *V* of your hitting hand. Hold your right hand out in front of you with the fingers spread and the back of the hand facing you—as though admiring your fingernails. Scrutinize the area where your thumb protrudes strangely out to the left of your index finger. Take special note of that web of skin connecting the bases of your thumb and index finger. This should look like the webbing between the toes of your pet frog. Now for the fun part. Start bringing your thumb and index finger closer together without bending them. Observe your frog's toe-web crack a vertical smile when thumb and index finger are at about a thirty-degree angle. Well, smile back, because you have formed the V— the point of reference for the forehand (and, in chapter 6, the backhand) grip.

The V at the juncture of the thumb and index finger goes right on the middle of the uppermost flat surface of the handle when you grasp the racquet properly for the forehand. Reread that last sentence because it is the basis for this step and for the whole forehand grip. Grip the racquet in this manner now.

If the V does not fall on the center of the upper handle surface, you are holding on with

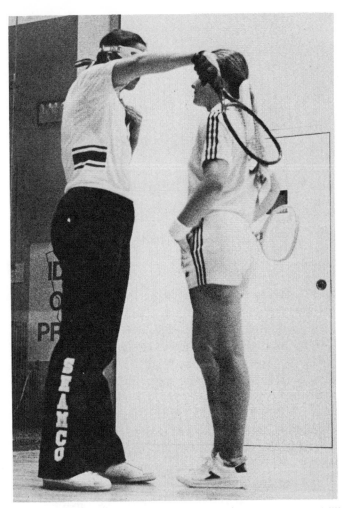

"Look, *you* hold the racquet the way you want and *I'll* hold the racquet the way I want." When getting a lesson on how to grip the racquet—whether it be from another person or from an instructional book—it is best to have an actual racquet in hand instead of just using your imagination. (Oram)

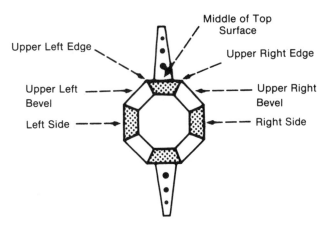

A butt view from the end of the racquet handle. For your forehand grip, the V formed by your thumb and index finger should fall approximately over the arrow labeled "middle of top surface."

The proper forehand grip begins when you grasp the throat of the racquet with your left hand.

Shake hands with the racquet handle. Your palm should lie along the right flat side of the handle.

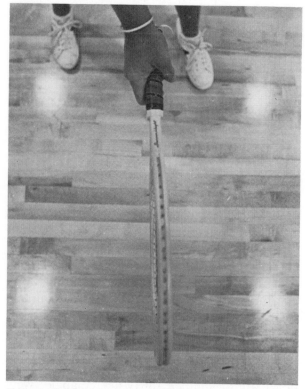

If the handle is properly rotated within your hand, the V formed by the juncture of your thumb and forefinger will fall directly over the middle of the topmost flat surface of the racquet handle. Squaring the racquet face to the front wall in this manner ensures solid straight-in shots.

an incorrectly rotated grip. That is, if the V falls too far to the right of the middle of the upper surface, you are behind the racquet handle—as in the previously described Neanderthal club grip. Go ahead, and for a minute hold the racquet improperly with this behind-the-handle grasp. Hold that grip and—without the ball—

take a practice forehand swing. Stop the swing in midstroke, where you normally contact the ball. Note that the racquet face slants down toward the floor—the face is closed.

On the other hand, the V at the base of your thumb and index finger may fall too far the opposite way. It may be improperly positioned to the left of the middle of the upper surface of the handle. That spells just as bad trouble when you start swinging. Take a practice swing as before—without the ball—and stop in midstroke where you normally contact the ball. Note that at this freeze position the racquet slants up toward the ceiling—the face is open. It isn't hard to predict that shots with this incorrect grip will angle upward.

I dwell on the V point of reference because it is perhaps the most important yet least understood aspect of the grip. If your shots consistently angle either too low or too high off the racquet strings, first suspect an overly closed or open face, respectively. This can usually be traced back to a misplaced frog's toe smile on the grip.

5. I have repeatedly refuted the fist grip but have not yet provided the correct alternative. The proper technique is termed the trigger finger grip.

Grasp the racquet as outlined by all the steps above. Now move your index finger up slightly on the handle so that a small space appears between your index and middle fingers. The knuckles of these two fingers should be about a half inch apart. This is called the trigger finger or pistol grip because it resembles pulling the

Avoid an improper fist grip by moving your index finger up on the handle slightly so that there is a small space between your index and middle fingers.

Rest the index finger back on the handle. This is the correct trigger-finger grip, in which the knuckles of your index and middle fingers are about half an inch apart. The trigger-finger grip gives greater racquet control since it allows more of your hand to cover more of the handle surface.

Check to make sure that the butt of the racquet lies approximately against the heel of your hand.

trigger of a pistol when you play cops and robbers.

Big deal, you say, just what does it accomplish? This minute adjustment allows the hand to cover at least 10 percent more surface area of the handle. The extra surface area covered includes the upper portion of the handle, which is where racquet control originates. Therefore, the trigger finger increases swing control.

6. Now check to see that you are gripping the racquet at the proper height on the handle. Look at the butt. It should rest in the heel of your hand.

To locate the heel of your hand, look at your palm. The heel is that fleshy pad on the left lower quadrant of your right palm. You're going to find, as I have, that if you run around the courts long enough with the butt on your heel, a callus forms on that fleshy hump. Yep, you'll witness a little mound of hard flesh pop up on that area of your palm and proudly announce, "I belong to the hand of a racquetball fanatic!"

Placing the butt of the racquet in the heel of your hand is intended only as a general guide to grip height. This guide has evolved from the ups and downs of both ends of the racquet handle. I remember that during the old days of dead balls and tinker toy racquets the grip gospel, according to the experts, demanded that you hold the racquet as low on the handle as possible. Your little finger, it was said, should run off the end of the handle—as though you were daintily holding a teacup according to proper etiquette. I suppose there was a reason for this low grip at the time. Back then, if you choked up much higher on the handle, you lost the leverage necessary to propel the slower balls with the less potent racquets. This, then, was the era of the eagle-claw grip. But the grip moved up toward the other end of the handle with the advent of the superfast ball. Now the instructing demigods preached a new gospel: you must choke up on the handle a half inch to an inch, or suffer the consequence of lessened control. This, then, was the era of the Ping-Pong grip.

I believe these were as much errors as eras. Let's call today—and what I am teaching here— the era of the butt-in-heel grip. It is a compromise between the two previous grip eras. Note, again, that this compromise grip is a guide rather than a stringent mandate. It has about a

This series of photos shows the effect of racquet handle rotation on the angle of the racquet face for forehand shots. The grip in this photo *(above left)* has the thumb–index finger V too far to the right (too near the right bevel of the top handle surface). The result? . . .

. . . the racquet face is too closed, or it angles down at the floor at the point of ball contact. Shots hit using this improper grip go into the floor with excess top spin *(above center).*

Here the thumb–index finger V *(above right)* lies too far to the left on the handle (too near the left bevel of the handle's top surface). The result? . . .

. . . the racquet face is too open, or it angles upward at the point of ball contact. You can see that shots hit with this improper grip *(below left)* will angle too high into the front wall with excess back spin.

This, the correct racquet rotation *(below center),* places the thumb–index finger V right over the middle of the topmost flat surface of the handle. The result? . . .

. . . the racquet face is properly perpendicular to the floor *(below right).*

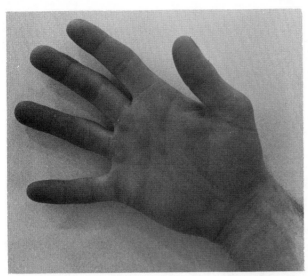

You can often identify veteran racquetballers by the callus on the fleshy hump of the heel of the hand. The butt of the racquet goes approximately against the heel of the hand when gripping the handle for both forehand and backhand shots.

half inch of tolerance, which allows you to grip up or down the handle a half inch from the exact butt-in-heel position. Your final grip within this half inch of tolerance should reflect your personal comfort and stroke results.

Important note: Be advised not to deviate too far up or down the handle on your grip, unless you've been around the game a long time. Remember the recommended half inch of tolerance either way. The higher up you grip the handle—in the direction of the Ping-Pong grip—the more control but the less power you have. If you choose to experiment upward on the han-

dle, fine. Go up an eighth of an inch at first and see what happens when you hit a few balls. Then, if you must, continue up by one-eighth-inch increments—up to half an inch above the normal heel-in-butt grip. The same rule holds when you experiment with your grip in the reverse direction—down the handle. Go toward the eagle-claw grip only an eighth of an inch at a time, pausing at each increment to hit enough shots to get a feel for that particular grip height. You should find that the lower you grip the racquet, the more power but the less control you have.

I can sense that you're skeptical that such a minor adjustment in grip height could cause such an appreciable difference in the control-power mix on your swings. A practical analogy here should convince you. Recall the last time you used a hammer to pound a nail. You started out by grasping the handle fairly high toward the head, and used short controlled hits to get the nail started without banging your thumb. Once the nail was started, you shifted your grip on the hammer a little toward the end of the handle and pounded the nail a few more times until it stuck stably about halfway into the wood. Then, if the nail was long, you adjusted your grip to hold the hammer at the very end of the handle, and you issued the final few powerful blows. You may have missed the nail entirely with a couple of these final swings, but when you hit it, it really moved.

The same effect takes place with the racquet and ball. But don't just read it here, nod your

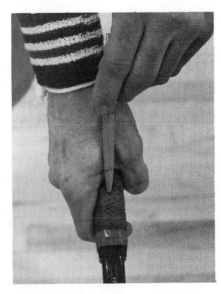

The thumb-forefinger V juncture is the prime locater for racquetball grips. Grab a racquet and note the web of skin connecting the bases of your thumb and index finger. This web forms a V as you grasp the racquet.

The V for the forehand grip goes directly over the middle of the top-most surface of the handle. The pen in this photo points at the middle of the topmost surface.

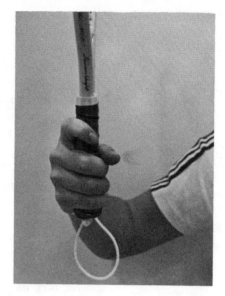

A side view of the trigger-finger grip reveals the small space between the index and middle fingers.

. . . a view from underneath the handle. This emphasizes the importance of the trigger finger when you grip the racquet.

head in agreement, and say "What a brilliant analogy!" Try it out right now—with the racquet and ball. Go up and down the handle in eighth-inch increments and take mental note of the effect on power and control.

7. The final step for the forehand grip concerns how tightly to grip the racquet. There is really no empirical measure, as could be applied with the previous steps. Grip tightness is relative according to your squeeze strength. But, if you must have a more precise monitor of grip tightness, try using about 80 percent of your maximum squeeze when you are gripping to swing at the ball. That is, grasp the racquet with about the same degree of tightness as when you shake hands with an opponent before a match—firmly and with confidence.

Perhaps more significant than how much is when to squeeze down on the handle. You should grasp the racquet firmly when hitting the ball, then loosen your clasp slightly until it is your turn to swing again. This process should be natural and unconscious—squeeze, relax, squeeze, relax, as the rally continues. If you ever come across a player who constantly grasps her racquet in a white-knuckle grip—even when her opponent is hitting the ball—you can logically conclude that you are witnessing an intense individual in an intense game. Her forearm will cramp into the texture of a frozen potato if the game continues much longer at that level of stress.

Let's review the seven steps to the proper forehand grasp.

1. Hold the racquet by the throat in front of you with your nongun hand.

2. Shake hands with the racquet handle with your hitting hand.

3. Check that your palm and the right flat surface of the handle lie in the same plane—perpendicular to the floor.

4. Place the thumb-index finger V on the center of the uppermost handle surface to ensure proper rotation.

5. Use a trigger-finger grip with a small space between the knuckles of your index and middle fingers.

6. Place the butt of the racquet into the heel of your hand.

7. Grasp the racquet firmly and with authority when you hit the ball.

COMMON ERRORS

After you feel you have the forehand grip down pat, I suggest you evaluate it with the checklist below. Then, have a knowledgeable person make a final inspection. This may all seem redundant until you consider the other possibility. Suppose you practice hundreds of forehand strokes a day for the next month, only to discover at the end of that time that your grip has been wrong. How sad, especially since it is more difficult to correct an improper grip than it is to learn the proper grip the first time. And worse, altering the grip almost always involves a concurrent change in the stroke. So, let's carefully examine the typical grip errors.

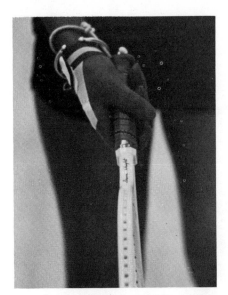

Common error number one for the forehand grip is grasping behind the handle, or with the V too far to the right on the handle surface. This very common mistake causes . . .

. . . the racquet face to slant down at the floor (closed face) at the potential point of forehand contact.

1. Common error number one is grasping the racquet behind the handle. In other words, the thumb-index finger V falls too far to the right on the uppermost flat surface of the handle. In extreme improper cases, the V may fall on the right flat surface (the one parallel with the racquet face) rather than on the uppermost one.

Grab your racquet now in this incorrect manner just to see how it feels and how much it closes the racquet face. Suspect this common error if your stroke feels comfortable but your shots consistently skip into the floor. This error often goes hand in hand with the improper fist grip, which is explained below.

Common error number two. In this photo, the face of the racquet is too open. It is caused by grasping the handle with the V too far to the left on the uppermost surface (too close to the left bevel).

Common error number three is the fist grip. Avoid this by checking that: (1) your thumb-index finger V falls over the middle of the topmost surface, and (2) your hand is spread over the handle with a trigger-finger grip.

2. Much less common an error is grasping the racquet too far to the left—in the opposite direction of the previous error. When the V falls too far to the left on the handle's uppermost surface, the racquet face opens too much and your forehands don't feel solid upon ball contact. Your shots will likely come off the strings with power-dampening slice, or backspin. Another symptom of this error is having shots consistently go too high into the front wall.

Among improper grippers, I'd estimate that only one player grips with the V too far left (open face) for every five players who grip with the V too far right (closed face).

3. This error is the fist grip described earlier as the Neanderthal grasp. It often occurs in conjunction with the behind-the-handle mis-grip described in error number one. Be aware that your racquet is neither a tenpin nor a cave woman's club. If you hold it as such, you'll likely skip a majority of your kill attempts into the floor. In addition, you'll have less racquet

control with the fist grip. This is because, as I pointed out before, your palm covers less handle surface. Players who use a fist grip might as well have a missing index finger on the hand -that grasps the racquet handle. Spread it out a tad with a trigger finger grip.

4. Grasping the racquet too high is an error that, for some mysterious reason, is especially prevalent among female players. The major symptom of this problem is a lack of power. Recall that the higher on the handle you hold the racquet, the less leverage you have. Do you swing a real mean stroke but your shots nonetheless lack pizzazz? You may be too choked up.

5. Less common among female players than choking up is holding the handle too low on the racquet. The main symptom here is random rubber bullets—your shots have warp velocity but no accuracy. The cure? Try choking up on the handle in eighth-inch increments until you feel in control of your racquet.

Common error number four is grasping the racquet too high on the handle. Choking too far up in this manner leads to a loss of stroke power. It is allowable to choke up a little on the handle, but don't let the heel of your hand stray too far above the butt of the racquet.

Common error number five is holding the racquet too low on the handle. Moving too far down on the handle in this manner does increase stroke power through additional leverage (if you can still snap your wrist just as fast on the swing), but this is a trade-off in that you'll experience a decrease in racquet control. Keep your little finger on the handle and avoid the eagle-claw grip.

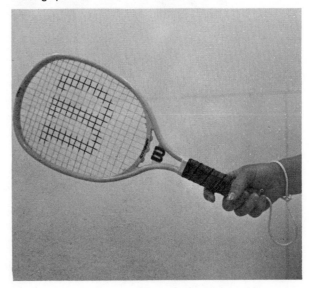

Rich Wagner has an outstanding forehand, and most of his pro opponents wisely choose to play to his back-hand side. Note here some of the important add-ons that comprise a formidable forehand kill shot: contact below the knees, wrist snap (the racquet blur) at ball contact, a hitting depth just behind the heel of the lead foot, and weight transfer from rear to front foot during the downswing. The result? A 110-mile-per-hour roll off. (Leach)

5
Forehand Stroke

I expect you now have a basic grasp of the forehand grip that is fairly close to the model grip presented in the previous chapter. Again, I don't demand exact imitation of every technique this book offers, since each of us has anatomical idiosyncrasies that make such exact conformity impractical. However, at least with the grips, adhere closely to the models. Otherwise, the instruction in this and the backhand stroke chapter will be useless.

I require less strict imitation of the models with the strokes than with the grips. Therefore, take the model forehand that I'm about to unveil as a general guide. Merge it into what feels comfortable and right for you. Otherwise, you'll end up with the unnatural jerky swing of a programmed robot.

The following presentation of the forehand is

similar to the trampoline game called *add-on*. In add-on there are two people, each bouncing on a trampoline. One person does an easy trick such as a seat drop, which is a simple bounce on the hind end. The other person then does the seat drop, perhaps followed by a stomach, in which she bounces on her tummy. Then the first person might do a seat drop, a stomach drop, and then a backflip. The two gymnasts continue in this manner—adding on one trick at a time— until one person cannot execute the sequence of movements. Back in my high school gymnastic days, we might get up to twenty add-on tricks in a row before somebody goofed.

Get ready for racquetball add-on. My add-on learning method for the stroke is easier and requires fewer tricks than in gymnastics. You will not goof, though you may get temporarily bogged down on one particular add-on within the string of movements. No problem—just work on that trouble spot until you get it down pat, then go on to the next add-on. I emphasize that each movement is a building block upon which the ensuing ones build. Get each add-on right before continuing. Also, don't skip over any add-on because it seems too simple or worthless. One link in this chain of movements may be less significant than another, but all the links are required if a stroke chain is to exist in the end.

In this add-on manner, you will quickly accumulate the basic movements that comprise the model forehand stroke. And it's fun, since it *is* kind of a game.

FOREHAND ADD-ONS

The following steps are intentionally simple and straightforward. They are geared toward the beginning player who has had little swing time on the court, or toward the intermediate whose swing time is perhaps a tad arhythmic. I'm not apologizing. I'm merely saying that advanced players may find these add-ons overly simplistic. These players should stifle their yawns and quickly run through the series of add-ons anyway. Even advanced racquetballers must admit to having less than perfect strokes, or they wouldn't be reading this in the first place. And besides, this add-on series can be used to ferret out the weak link(s) in the chain of movements called the forehand. On with the add-ons.

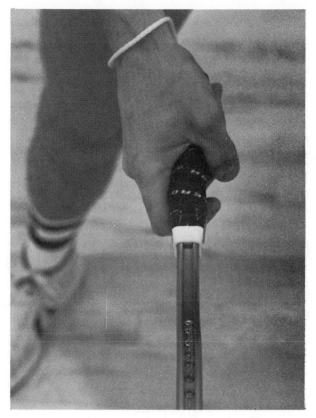

Add-on 1. Start with the proper forehand grip.

The starting stance for the series of forehand add-ons is approximately on the short line facing the right sidewall. Your feet should be nearly parallel to each other and point at that sidewall. As you become more experienced and hit the ball harder, you may move this starting stance deeper in the court.

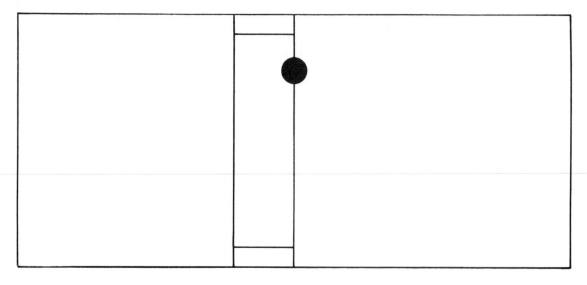

1. Grip your racquet with the correct forehand grip.

2. Stand on the court facing the right sidewall so that when you reach out your arm and racquet the end of your racquet is about three feet from the sidewall. Your toes therefore point at, and are about six feet from, the sidewall. How deep in the court? You should straddle the short line—the second horizontal red line from the front wall.

3. Now close your stance. First, let me explain the difference between the closed stance and the open stance. Let's assume you are standing facing the right sidewall, as described in step two. As you gradually open your stance, your lead (left) foot moves more toward the center of the court. Simultaneously, your left toe points more and more at the front wall until your tennis shoe points rudely at the left front corner. An open stance on the forehand is undesirable, as you will see.

Now let's close the stance, which is what this step is all about. Forget about the open stance

and resume your original position, facing the right sidewall as described in step two. As you gradually close your stance, your left foot moves more to the right and front. Consequently, your left toe points more and more at, and gets closer and closer to, the right sidewall. Soon the eyelets of your Buster Browns are looking straight ahead at that sidewall. Your right toe is still six feet from the right sidewall, but your left toe is now only about four feet away. All this fancy stance stuff boils down to this: a closed stance for the forehand has the lead foot about two feet closer to the right sidewall than the rear foot. (This rule of foot will also hold when we take up stances for the backhand stroke in chapter 7.)

Okay, go ahead and close your stance by sliding your left foot about two feet closer to the sidewall than your right foot. I say *about* two feet closer because the precise distance that your lead foot moves depends largely on your height. You'll slide a few inches more or less depending on whether you're a giraffe or a dachshund, respectively and respectfully.

Now try a little body awareness. How does it

Add-on 2. Stand on the short line facing the right sidewall.

Add-on 3. Close your stance by sliding your lead (left) foot about two feet closer to the sidewall.

feel to be in a closed stance? If you still feel conspicuously upright, then close your stance a few more inches by sliding your left foot closer to the right sidewall. However, if your legs feel uncomfortably spread like a flamingo doing a split, then close your stance a little less by a few inches by sliding your left foot away from the right sidewall. Are you comfortable now? Good, try the body awareness routine again to get the feel of this closed stance. It is important to recognize the feeling of the closed stance because it is the basis of the rest of the forehand stroke.

If you seek instruction elsewhere, you are liable to run into opposition to this concept of using a closed stance on racquetball strokes. I am talking about stepping into the ball in a closed stance (as will be explained) versus the traditional step into the ball, which has been more toward an open stance. That is, players have been taught to step forward and at the front wall to initiate the swing. Sorry, but this tradition is about to crumble. Why (I can hear tradition asking) must I crumble? Why must I defer to the closed stance? There are many reasons.

First, the step toward the right sidewall (and toward a closed stance) on the forehand gives a potentially more powerful stroke than the step toward the front wall (and toward a more open stance). The rationale behind this can be proven theoretically and in actual play, but it is beyond the scope of this book. I suggest you try both

methods to convince yourself that the closed stance generates greater swing power.

Second, you get an additional negative effect when you hit the ball from an open stance. The step that opens the hips and shoulders toward the front wall almost forces your body to pull the shot crosscourt. This is similar to the tendency of a baseball batter to pull a ball into left field. You will learn that, strategically speaking, most racquetball shots (especially kills) should go up and down the line rather than crosscourt. The step toward the closed stance encourages the body to hit the ball straight in and up and down the line.

There are also several subtle advantages to hitting the ball from a closed stance. Better ball spin and added deception are just two examples. But these are complex issues, again too deep for this instruction. You'd only get bogged down in confusion and lose sight of the more relevant points if I attempted an explanation of these.

Are you still unconvinced, or does stepping into this closed stance still feel horribly uncomfortable? Then try compromising between my closed stance and the traditional open stance. That is, step somewhere between a direction at the sidewall and a direction at the front wall. This means stepping at the right front corner to initiate your forehand swing.

4. You're now in the closed stance, as though you just stepped into the ball. Next, extend your arm and racquet toward the right sidewall and

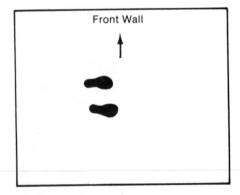

The incorrect open stance for the forehand has your lead (left) foot no closer to the right sidewall than your rear (right) foot. But . . .

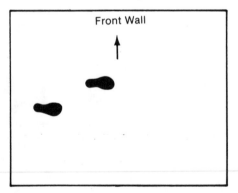

. . . the correct closed stance for the forehand has your lead foot about two feet closer to the right sidewall than is your rear foot. This proper closed stance provides more stroke power and encourages down-the-line shots.

cock your wrist. That is, lay the wrist and the racquet handle up and back. You probably wonder what the directions *up* and *back* mean. Let's try it. First you'll do the up-and-back wrist cock without a racquet, then you'll do the same with a racquet in hand. To cock your wrist without the racquet, follow the steps below:

Add-on 4. Extend your arm and racquet toward the right sidewall and cock your wrist up and back.

The forehand wrist cock is a laying up and back of the wrist, though the more significant part is the laying back. To lay your wrist back into the cocked position (without the racquet), extend your arm and hand in front of you *(top right)* . . .

. . . point your fingers at the ceiling *(center right)* as though waving hello, and . . .

. . . now just rotate your hands *(right)* so the fingers point at the right rear corner (assuming you are facing the right sidewall).

Recall that you have done all this without a racquet in hand. Remember also that your arm has remained stiff as a board and extended straight out fron your body toward the right sidewall. Only your wrist has angled up and back at its hinged joint. Your fingers, like five fleshy chopsticks, are still unbent. Maintain the final wrist cock position for thirty seconds to become aware of how it feels.

Now add the racquet and go through the previous illustrated steps. Hold the final wrist cock for thirty seconds. (Is your forehand grip still correct?)

The laying back of the wrist for the wrist cock on the forehand with the racquet follows the same three-step sequence: point the racquet away from you with the strung surface parallel with the ceiling . . .

. . . point the racquet at the ceiling, and . . .

. . . rotate your hand so that the racquet points back. Your wrist and racquet are now cocked back, the more important half of the forehand back-and-up wrist cock.

Remember that, besides cocking your wrist back at the top of the forehand backswing, you should also cock it up. Thus, the head of your racquet will point slightly toward the top of your own head instead of pointing directly up at the ceiling.

5. You are now feeling rather foolish—in a closed stance, your right arm extended toward the right sidewall, the racquet in your mitt, and your wrist cocked. From this position, take your racquet back with a one-foot backswing. Got it? No, that's too far. Only a one-foot backswing, maintaining your wrist cock. Got it? No, your backswing is going up, instead of back toward the back wall and parallel to the floor.

This, then, is the beginning of the forehand backswing. I know it feels strange, but please bear with the add-ons.

6. From the one-foot backswing position described in the previous step, now flick your wrist forward toward the front wall so that your wrist snaps in front of you and so you follow through past the wrist snap only by one foot. Do it again, starting with the one-foot backswing. I emphasize that this two-foot swing (one foot of backswing and one foot of follow-through) must be parallel to the floor.

Do you remember Magnolia Morepower who tried to swing with no backswing and no follow-through? Well, your swing should resemble hers if you're performing this step correctly. However, you have a two-foot swing, whereas poor Maggie had none. And she wondered why she didn't have more power!

Repeat step six without a ball about twenty times.

7. Now add the ball to this abbreviated stroke. Bounce the ball on the floor at a spot

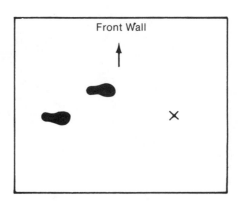

The spot (X) on the floor where you bounce the ball for the drop and hit is important. The ball should bounce about a foot behind and two feet out from your front foot (after you have stepped into the stroke).

about one foot behind (toward the back wall) your lead foot, and about two feet out (toward the right sidewall) from your lead foot.

The depth of contact here—one foot behind your lead foot—is constant whatever your physiotype. The reach for the ball—about two feet out from your lead foot—is somewhat variable. If you are tall and gangly, you may want to add six inches or so to the distance from your body at which you contact the ball. On the other hand, if you're a fire hydrant in gym shorts, you may want to decrease this distance by about six inches.

Before you make any gross adjustments to these two dimensions, I hasten to add that the dimensions pinpointing this spot at which you bounce the ball are not randomly conceived.

Add-on 5. Take the racquet into a horizontal one-foot backswing with your wrist still cocked.

Add-on 6. Use a one-foot backswing and snap your wrist.

Add-on 7. Bounce the ball *(top)* about one foot behind and two feet out from your lead foot. Then catch the ball just after it peaks at knee height *(above)*. The place you catch the ball is your point of contact when you start hitting.

The forehand wrist flick (with or without a racquet) is *(top left)* a forceful flexion of the hand at the wrist joint *(center left)*, as though you were slapping someone across the face *(left)*. Try it. Also try this wrist flick with a racquet in hand.

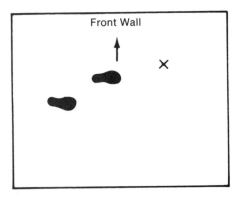

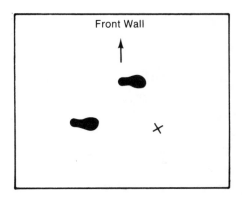

If you bounce and contact the ball too far forward, you lose power and will likely pull most of your shots crosscourt.

On the other hand, if you bounce and contact the ball too deep in your stance, you'll have trouble snapping your wrist in time for ball contact, and your forehand shots probably will glance feebly into the right sidewall.

Look at what happens when you deviate too far from my recommendations: Contact the ball farther forward, and you'll likely pull most of your shots crosscourt. Contact the ball any deeper in the stance, and you'll probably get only glancing blows that angle the ball into the right sidewall. Contact the ball too close to your body and you'll jam your swing, which means that you lose the smooth pendulum swing arc. In addition, the ball picks up excess spin and you lose power. Contact the ball too far away from your body, and you may become off balance during your follow-through. (These four mistakes relating to the position of ball contact will be covered in greater detail in chapter 9.)

How high should you bounce the ball? Make it peak at knee height. Now you've got all the dimensions—the spot on the floor to bounce the ball and how high to bounce it. Do it, and catch the ball just after it peaks. Do not hit it yet. Repeat twenty times or until your bounces are consistent.

The classic forehand wrist cock—up and back. Also note Steve Strandemo's high and deep backswing and his eagle-eye concentration. (Bledsoe)

Add-on 8. Bounce and hit the ball in your contact zone just after it peaks at knee height. Use a one-foot backswing and a one-foot follow-through to wrist flick the ball at the front wall.

Aim your forehand shots on these add-ons at an area on the front wall that is knee- to waist-high and two or three feet from the right sidewall. Concentrate initially more on stroke form and power than on accuracy. The accuracy will come naturally as you hit more and more shots.

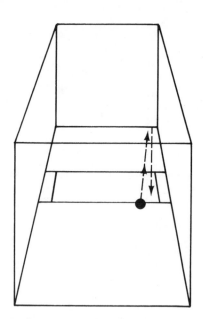

8. You finally get to hit the ball on this step. The previous steps have brought you to a position in which you are in a closed stance, your arm is back in a one-foot backswing, your wrist is cocked up and back, and the ball is bouncing up to your contact zone.

The contact zone is the area where you normally contact the ball. This is analogous to the strike zone in baseball. The batter belts the baseball when it enters her strike zone. You belt the racquetball when it enters your contact zone. In the previous step I described the very center of your contact zone as a spot that is knee high, about a foot behind the lead foot and about two feet out from the lead foot. Again, that is the precise center of the zone. The area or zone in which you may successfully hit the ball with your racquet is larger than this by some inches in all directions from the exact center. The better your stroke, the larger your contact zone. This is why pro players get away with hitting kills at a height and depth of contact that is ridiculous for most players even to consider. In sum, the closer to the center of the contact zone you hit the ball, the more power and accuracy you will have.

As I said, in this step you hit the ball just after it peaks at the center of your contact zone. Hence, this step is exactly the same as step six, in which you took the two-foot swing (one foot of backswing and one foot of follow-through). Now, however, you hit the ball with a flick of your wrist. Your swing is still horizontal, or parallel to the floor.

Don't fret about your accuracy right now. Just aim for an area on the front wall that is knee- to waist-high and a couple of feet from the right sidewall. The ball should rebound off the front wall and right back at you. Catch it. If it doesn't rebound straight back to you, chase it. Repeat until the ball does come back so that you don't have to run all over the place to catch it.

Are you having trouble limiting your backswing and follow-through to one foot each? Try a brick wall. Really, just imagine a vertical brick wall one foot behind the point of ball contact. You obviously can draw your backswing back only to this wall. Also envision another vertical brick wall about one foot forward of your point of contact. This limits your follow-through. Thus, the two brick walls are parallel and two feet apart. If your backswing or follow-through exceeds these, you'll no doubt end up with a racquet having an imaginary broken frame.

Don't worry about stroke power yet either, because I'm intentionally limiting you to a short backswing and follow-through that allow no more than a wrist flick. This is not to deny the power of the wrist. At clinics I frequently demonstrate the power that is packed solely in the wrist snap with a quick series of hits. I prelude them by saying, "I'm going to hit the ball with only about a foot of backswing and a foot of follow-through. I'll use no body, no weight transfer, and I won't step into the ball on this hit." Then I drop and wrist flick the ball into the front wall at about forty miles per hour.

The point of contact has three dimensions: distance from body, depth, and height. In this photo note that the first dimension is alluded to—you should bounce the ball comfortably away from your body.

The second dimension, the depth of contact, is indicated here by the line—just behind the heel of your lead foot. This photo also shows the third dimension—height. Contact your kill strokes at knee height or lower whenever possible.

Add-on 9. The wrist flick in this step starts with a two-foot cocked backswing.

"That shot," I tell them, "is just to demonstrate the power of the wrist. It isn't supposed to be a correct swing just yet. Now look at what happens when I take a full backswing and follow-through." Then I add a good backswing and follow-through to the wrist flick when I drop and hit. The ball picks up quite a bit of steam, hitting the front wall at, say, sixty miles per hour. Finally, I say to the clinic group, "Look at what happens now when I add body rotation, weight transfer, and a step forward to the string of stroke movements up to now." Then I knock their eyes out with a hundred-mile-per-hour smasheroo at the front wall. This demonstration begins with just a simple wrist flick—that nucleus of stroke power.

Perform this step—the bounce and flick

drill—twenty times or however many it takes for you to get the hang of it.

9. This step is a piece of cake. You're going to add a little power by adding an extra foot of backswing and an extra foot of follow-through.

Drop and flick the ball at knee height from the closed stance, as in the previous step. But this time start with a two-foot backswing and end with a two-foot follow-through. That gives you a whopping four-foot swing. Don't take any more just yet. Mentally construct the parallel brick walls again—one two feet behind the point of ball contact to limit your backswing, and the other two feet ahead of the point of contact to stop your follow-through.

Your backswing and follow-through must be

A picture-perfect forehand frozen an instant before contact. The ball is dropping to below knee height, the downswing has begun with a beautiful wrist cock, the lead leg is crossed over in a closed stance, and the weight transfer is occurring—from rear to front foot. The elbow leads the wrist that leads the racquet right up to the moment of contact. Combine all of these exemplary stroke mechanics with excellent eye contact and concentration, and Lynn Adams is virtually assured of hitting a winner. (Charfauros)

absolutely level and parallel to the floor for now. No lift or swoop is allowed. Pretend there is a tabletop that runs knee-high and parallel to the floor all along the bottom of your horizontal stroke. Your racquet cannot penetrate—go below—this table. Also pretend there is an upper limiting barrier. This is another tabletop (an upside-down table) running a foot above and parallel to the lower table. In other words, these two tabletops limit the altitude of your swing arc to knee height from the beginning of your two-foot backswing to the end of your two-foot follow-through.

Practice this step twenty times, or until you feel ready to add on.

10. This is the same as the previous step, only you now take a three-foot backswing and a three-foot follow-through. Your wrist should now have room to snap much more forcefully upon ball contact (no longer just a flick). This snap, plus the increased total swing distance (six feet), should greatly increase your power.

Remember that your stance is still closed. There is no step into the ball. Contact is at knee height just after the ball peaks in the center of the contact zone. Your swing is parallel to the floor throughout. Flick-hit the ball and retrieve, flick-hit and retrieve, twenty times or more. Don't break your racquet on the brick walls and don't trip over the tables.

11. This is the same as the previous step, but now you get to take your maximum backswing and follow-through. Your maximum is whatever depth of backswing and follow-through that feels right and comfortable, as long as you remain within the upper and lower tabletop barriers. In other words, the brick walls have been removed, but the tables remain.

From the very back of your backswing with the wrist cocked, your racquet should sweep level at knee height throughout the stroke and follow-through. Don't worry about the distance of your follow-through, as long as it remains horizontal and doesn't jerk to a premature stop

Add-on 10. Drop and flick-hit the ball, using a three-foot backswing and a three-foot follow-through.

Add-on 11. Take as deep a backswing as feels comfortable. The wrist still starts cocked at the top of the backswing and snaps at ball contact. In addition, the entire stroke is still fairly horizontal.

Add-on 12. Start your backswing with a ninety-degree crook at your elbow. Your forearm points up at the ceiling and your wrist is cocked up and back.

right after you hit the ball. This stroke is now similar to slapping someone across the face. There is an analogous backswing, wrist cock, level swing to the contact area, wrist snap at the point of contact, and level follow-through. Just pretend the ball has a face, then slap it with the racquet.

Let's review this step. The ready position is with the racquet cocked at the back of your maximally comfortable backswing. Bounce the ball so it peaks at knee level and, as usual, stroke it with a good wrist snap in the contact zone. The shot should travel about knee-high into the front wall and rebound back to you. Catch or retrieve it, and repeat at least twenty times.

12. Now let's transform your backswing and follow-through into a more realistic stroke. It entails only a simple add-on—a truer-to-form backswing. Start the stroke as in the previous step, with your hitting arm straight back and parallel to the floor in the cocked backswing

position. Freeze right there. Now crook your elbow to a ninety-degree angle. The tricep-bicep portion of your upper arm is still parallel to the floor, but your forearm (from elbow to wrist) should point straight up at the ceiling. Your wrist is still cocked up and back. The face of the racquet should lie in about the same plane as your shoulders.

Feel better? Take a hefty swipe at the ball. The only difference from the previous step is that we've removed the upper limiting table at the top of your backswing. Though your backswing starts higher than before, your stroke should flatten out at knee height. The imaginary lower tabletop is still intact so that your swing must sweep along this up to and after ball contact.

You now have one full piece of the model forehand stroke—the backswing. Once again, the top of the backswing has the triceps approximately parallel to the floor, the elbow crooked at about ninety degrees, and the forearm pointing directly at the ceiling. Hit twenty or more shots. Then add on.

This short photo sequence illustrates what to do after setting your feet to hit the ball in a game situation. First, raise your racquet as you eyeball the oncoming sphere.

Cock your wrist.

Your elbow leads your cocked wrist and racquet during the downswing.

This photo sequence at the right, below, and on the opposite page shows what your stroke should look like up to and including add-on 12. Note that this is basically the forehand stroke minus the step into the ball and minus the body rotation on the backswing.

Other points to ponder: Note my crooked elbow at the top of the backswing. My wrist flicks so the racquet hits the ball just after the peak of its bounce—slightly below my knees. My follow-through is relatively flat because my swing has been fairly horizontal—parallel to the floor.

13. You have not stepped into the ball up to this point. This may have felt awkward, especially if you have ever thrown or hit any kind of ball in any sport at all. Let's take care of that awkwardness with this step.

Start with the previous step, with the racquet cocked in the crooked backswing ready position—but now do not assume a closed stance. Instead, begin with both feet parallel to each other and equidistant from the right sidewall. (This is precisely the same position outlined in step one of this chapter.) Okay, without the ball and without swinging your racquet, simply step into the closed stance. That's it, just step with your left foot—perhaps a little forward but mostly toward the right sidewall.

Freeze. You should now be back in the closed stance as per the last dozen steps, only with your racquet raised in the forehand ready position.

Repeat this movement again, starting in an open stance and then stepping into the closed stance. No swings and no balls yet. You're just learning how to step properly into the swing. Repeat twenty times.

14. Now you're going to add a racquet swing (without the ball) to the previous step. Start in an open stance with both feet approximately parallel and the same distance from the right sidewall. Your racquet is in a backswing position. Now begin your step into the closed stance

Add-on 13. Start in an open stance and . . .

. . . step into a closed stance. This add-on simulates stepping into a shot.

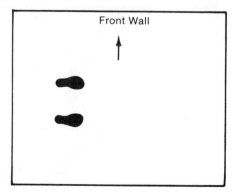

Front Wall

Add-on 14 is a simple step into an imaginary ball. You begin with your feet in an open stance and . . .

Add-on 14. Start with an open stance, step into a closed stance and swing at an imaginary ball.

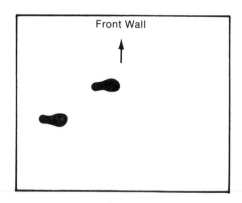

Front Wall

. . . step into a closed stance. Stepping into the ball ensures proper weight transfer during the downswing, which means added ball velocity after contact.

and, as soon as your stepping foot hits the floor, swing at an imaginary ball.

That's all there is to it. The trick is to get the step in synchrony with the swing. Don't use any body rotation on the backswing or follow-through yet. Step and swing, step and swing, repeating at least twenty times.

15. This step adds the ball to the previous step and swing. Start in an open stance with your racquet back in the cocked ready position as before. Then perform this sequence of movements:

Add-on 15. Bounce the ball so it will peak at knee height.

Step into a closed stance after the ball hits the floor.

Start your downswing as your lead foot hits the floor, and . . .

. . . hit the ball in the contact zone after it peaks just below your knees. No, or very little, body rotation yet—that comes in the next and final add-on.

I purposely ran together the movements in this step because this step is truly a run-on of add-ons. That is, one movement triggers another and another, like the laying down of dominoes. This should be a fluid sequence of motion rather than a jerky series of individual movements.

This is a very important step in our add-on game. It is also the first step that demands real timing, so don't be discouraged if your first few attempts are the staccato and mechanical movements of a robot operating on almost-drained batteries. The pauses and jerks will melt away with practice, and the individual movements will blend into a continuous motion. However, this may take more than twenty repetitions. Just keep telling yourself with each mistake on this step that patience is a virtue and persistence is divine.

16. We are at the end of the forehand add-ons that add up to the model stroke. Before tacking on the final step, run a mental check on these important points:

a. Is your wrist cocked up and back correctly?

b. Is your elbow crooked on the backswing?

c. Does your step into the stroke take you into a closed rather than an open stance?

d. Are you snapping your wrist forcefully at ball contact?

e. Is your swing fairly level and knee-high (as opposed to going in a big circle)?

f. Is your racquet handle nearly parallel to the floor (instead of pointing at the floor) when you contact the ball?

g. When you bounce the ball before swinging, does it hit the floor at the proper depth and distance from your lead foot? Does the ball peak at your knees?

Jennifer Harding wallops another one with great fore-hand form. It is difficult to tell if this is a serve or a stroke during the rally. Which would you say? I'd say it's either an awfully slow-moving ball during a rally, or she is foot-faulting right before the eyes of an unaware linesman. (Ektelon and Phillips Org.)

h. Is your whole stroke basically fluid, with add-on steps running imperceptibly together?

Now let's add on the final add-on in our model drop-and-hit stroke. This is the step in which you put body rotation into your swing. This means that the body coils on the backswing and uncoils on the downswing to provide explosive stroke power. Body rotation goes hand in hand with the step into the ball. These factors—the coil, the step, and the uncoil—ensure proper weight transfer. You've no doubt heard of this last term if you've participated in almost any kind of sport. In racquetball, weight transfer means that during the backswing the majority of your body weight rests on your rear foot, and during the follow-through the majority of that weight is shifted to the lead foot.

We may be getting bogged down here in obscure terms and nonspecifics. I'm going to use an analogy from baseball to illustrate the coil-step-uncoil that assures proper weight transfer. Consider the baseball batter receiving a pitched ball. As the ball comes at him he coils: He turns his pelvis slightly toward the catcher and simultaneously turns his shoulders even a bit more than his pelvis toward the catcher, also simultaneously shifting his body weight until most of it rests on his rear foot.

Add-on 16. The final add-on. Coil your hips and shoulders on the backswing, then . . .

The forehand windup. The actual start of the forehand is at the top (maximum) of the backswing. Hips and shoulders turn to face the right rear corner. This prepares you for . . .

. . . uncoil during the downswing. Body rotation is a major source of power on the stroke.

. . . the forehand follow-through after the hit. Hence, the termination of the forehand is at the end of the follow-through. Hips and shoulders have opened toward the front wall. Body weight has transferred from the back to front foot.

Let's freeze the image of that batter right there at the maximum body coil. The body coil before the swing is sometimes called body rotation or the windup. You can see that it is like tightening a spring, or cocking a gun, or like a rattlesnake coiling for the strike. All these build potential energy.

Let's get back to our baseball batter, who is still frozen in the maximum coil. As the baseball is about to enter the strike zone the batter uncoils explosively: His lead foot triggers the uncoil by stepping toward the pitcher—more toward first base for the racquetball stroke—which causes his hips to lead the uncoil by twisting forcefully around toward the pitcher. Simultaneously, his shoulders come around forcefully in the same direction as his hips, and then he swings the bat, which rides the surge of the powerful body uncoiling. Also simultaneously, his weight shifts almost entirely to his lead foot as he hits the ball.

That's the basic baseball swing, as well as the basic racquetball forehand swing—from the standpoint of body coil, stepping into the ball, and body uncoil. Note that this analogy has other parallels that are not directly related to weight transfer. There are analogous wrist cocks, wrist breaks, follow-throughs, and so on. But these items have already been covered in previous add-on steps. This step is concerned only with tapping the huge energy source of the body's bulk by coiling, stepping, and uncoiling.

You'll probably learn more about body rotation and weight transfer by doing it than by having me drone on about theories and analogies. So do it, with this final add-on for the forehand. Perform the same drop-and-hit motion as described in the previous step, but this time coil on your backswing and uncoil on your downswing. Pretend, if you wish, that you are a baseball batter, a human spring, or a rattlesnake in a T-shirt. Thus, the sequence for this step is as follows:

The Model Forehand: *(Below)* Bounce the ball *(left)* and your hips and shoulders should have a tendency to rotate *(center)*. Then begin to draw your racquet back to the backswing position *(right)*.

(Opposite) The ball should hit the floor so that it will peak in your contact zone *(top row, left)*. Just after the ball hits the floor, start your step into the closed stance *(center)*. The stride lengthens and the wrist cocks at the top of your backswing *(right)*.

Your lead foot hits the floor *(middle row, left)*, and your hips and shoulders begin to uncoil *(center)*. Your downswing starts to flatten out with your elbow leading your cocked wrist *(right)*.

The wrist snaps forcefully, which speeds the racquet head *(bottom row, left)* and now weight transfer is complete to the front foot *(center)*. The follow-through is fairly flat as the pelvis and shoulders continue to open to the front wall *(right)*.

This stroke sequence assumes you have been through all sixteen forehand add-ons. The emphasis in these photos is on a flat swing, which is dramatized here by a limiting horizontal surface under your stroke. This limiting barrier should serve to remind you that the head of your racquet should not dip or point down at the floor. Thus, the forehand swing is similar to a baseball pitcher throwing a ball sidearm, only with a racquet in hand. (Refer back to the sidearm throwing warm-up drill in chapter 3.)

That's it. Note that the racquetball stroke is a strength move as well as a speed move. It must be both forceful and fluid. Like a karate blow, it is a singular intense release of concentrated power and motion. Yet, the stroke must be less than an all-out flail or else you'll lose control and strain your arm. Obviously, this step is going to require some practice. Perform this final add-on until you feel coordinated and comfortable with the model forehand.

Other points to ponder in this photo: Note my weight shift from front to rear foot during the setup, then from rear to front foot during the downswing. Observe my body rotation at the top of the backswing, and my wrist cock at the beginning of the downswing. Try various degrees of these stroke components on your forehand.

The forehand follow-through. What can you say about my weight transfer and body rotation here? Remember that seeing is believing, but doing is learning. You'll discover more about body rotation and weight transfer from doing it in a court than from examining photos and reading explanations. (Charfauros)

SUMMARY OF ADD-ONS

It has been a lengthy trip through the forehand stroke add-ons. A road map might now prove helpful so you can remember where you've been and so you don't get lost when you return. Use the following summary of the forehand add-on steps as that road map.

1. Grip the racquet with the proper forehand grip.

2. Stand on the short line facing the right sidewall.

3. Close your stance by sliding your lead foot toward the right sidewall.

4. Extend your arm and racquet toward the right sidewall and cock your wrist up and back.

5. Take the racquet into a horizontal one-foot backswing with the wrist still cocked.

6. Take an abbreviated stroke without the ball, using a one-foot backswing and a one-foot follow-through.

7. Bounce the ball on the floor at a spot approximately one foot behind and two feet out from your lead foot. Catch rather than hit the ball just after it peaks at knee height.

8. Bounce and hit the ball in the center of the contact zone just after it peaks at knee height. Flick the ball at the front wall using the abbreviated stroke with a one-foot backswing and a one-foot follow-through.

9. Drop and wrist-flick the ball at the front wall using a stroke with a two-foot backswing and a two-foot follow-through.

10. Drop and flick-hit the ball using a stroke with a three-foot backswing and a three-foot follow-through.

11. Drop and hit the ball using your maximum comfortable backswing and follow-through. The entire stroke is still level and knee-high from backswing to follow-through.

12. Add a more realistic backswing to the stroke by crooking your elbow at ninety degrees, with your forearm pointing up at the ceiling.

13. Start with an open stance and step into a closed stance as though stepping into the ball. Do not swing yet.

14. Start with an open stance, step into a closed stance, and swing at an imaginary ball.

15. Step into and hit the ball.

16. Add body rotation—coil and uncoil of your hips and shoulders—to the swing to ensure proper weight transfer.

Steve Keeley has always been an advocate of the two-grip system for beginning players. The two-grip method of closing the racquet face slightly when hitting backhands is probably advantageous when a deader ball is used or when a control rather than a sheer power game is the primary goal. (Leach)

6
Backhand Grip

INTRODUCTION TO BACKHAND GRIP

The one-grip system or the two-grip system? That is, should you keep the same grip or should you change grips when going from a forehand to a backhand? This may be the most intriguing question since, "Is it true that no professional racquetball player has ever walked past a glass court without pausing to note his reflection?"

I won't hedge the issue. I feel the two-grip system, in which you use a slightly different grasp for the forehand and backhand strokes, is advantageous in a number of instances: when a deader ball is used, when a control style of game is the primary goal, or when the player doing the gripping is a beginner or an intermediate player. To the contrary, I believe the one-grip system (using the same grip for both the forehand and backhand strokes) is superior under other circumstances: when a livelier ball is used, when the primary objective is a power game, or when the player has been around the game long enough to have experienced both grip systems and their ramifications.

Let me state a few interesting facts to support and to expand upon the above points: (1) Almost all of the premier players in the old days of the deader balls utilized the two-grip method. (2) Almost all control players back then—and today—use the two-grip method. (3) More than half of today's top pro players use the one-grip method. (4) The majority of decent power players use the one-grip method. (5) None of the top one-grip players in racquetball's history has matched the control of the top two-grip players.

(6) None of the two-grip players in history has ever had the power of the one-grip players.

Let's delve into this a little further, since after you make a decision regarding which system to learn, you'll probably never change. The two-grip method works well with a mushy or slow ball on a solid (nonglass) court—where the ball floats around the court at a leisurely pace, where the rallies are longer and more controlled, and where the ball is very visible against solid walls. Each of these factors contributes to extra setup time on every shot. That is, the players have ample time to switch their grips from forehand to backhand and vice versa.

Now let's look at the other extreme, the conditions that favor the one-grip method. The one-grip system works well with a superball on a glass court—where the ball darts around the court like a berserk hummingbird, where the flailing rallies usually end quickly with kill shots, and where the players often visually lose the ball against the glass walls. These factors decrease the setup time players have on every shot of the rally. Decreased setup time precludes any sort of grip switch from forehand to backhand or vice versa.

Those are the pros and cons of the two schools of grip thought. But that's hedging, and I said that I wouldn't hedge on this matter. I recommend you use the two-grip system if you are a beginning to intermediate player who has no lofty aspirations of serious tournament play or of someday making a living as a racquetball pro. I emphasize this recommendation if you use a slower ball and prefer a controlled type of game. You have probably already deduced the basis for this advice. Beginning players have rallies that are slower and last longer, with the ball usually traveling at waist height rather than remaining constantly in a plane at shoestring level. This all allows more setup time—for the grip change. Furthermore, I advise such players to stay off glass courts, to work on their control game, and to use a slower nonpressurized ball (as suggested in chapter 2).

On the other hand, I recommend the one-grip system for experienced players whose racquetball objective goes beyond pure enjoyment. If you've already decided that you're going to set the hardwood world on fire someday, you might as well start tuning up for the power game.

Professional racquetball is brute power with a sprinkling of control. Start playing with a fast pressurized ball, work on the power serves (drives and hard Zs), and learn to kill the ball from any position on the court. And, of course, use the one-grip system.

Let's sidestep this theoretical muck now and grab a racquet. Got it? First we'll cover the backhand grip according to the two-grip system, then the backhand grip according to the one-grip system.

TWO-GRIP SYSTEM BACKHAND

We are going to proceed through the steps for the backhand grip just as we did earlier for the forehand grip. The explanation here will be briefer and easier to grasp because there will be some repetition from chapter 4. The backhand grip is essentially the same as the forehand grip (in this two-grip system), with one major difference: the placement of the thumb-index finger V on the handle is slightly altered, as will be explained.

First, grab your racquet and get a forehand grip, as described in chapter 4. Read over the following summary of the steps presented in that chapter if you are still unclear on the proper forehand grasp.

1. Hold the racquet with your left hand in front of your body at waist height. The strung face should be perpendicular to the floor.

2. Shake hands with the handle, using your right hand.

3. Your palm should rest against the right surface of the handle, both of which should be in the same plane, perpendicular to the floor.

4. The anatomical V juncture of your thumb and index finger goes on the middle of the uppermost handle surface. This assures proper rotation of the handle within your hand for the forehand.

5. Space your index and middle fingers slightly so that you have a trigger finger grip.

6. The butt of the handle end should fit comfortably into the fleshy heel of your hand.

7. Grip tightness is 80 percent of maximum squeeze when you swing at the ball.

Now for the one simple change from the forehand to the backhand grip. This adjustment concerns only step three, so all of the other

The pen marks the middle of the topmost surface of the handle. Since in this photo the thumb-index finger falls directly over where the pen points, this is the forehand grip.

The pen still points to the same place, but the V of the thumb-index finger is now to the left of the pen point. The V now lies over the left edge of the topmost surface, so this is the backhand grip.

steps remain the same. Holding the racquet with the proper forehand grip, now lightly grasp the bottom of the racquet frame with your left hand. You now use this off hand (left) to rotate the handle slightly within your right palm until you reach the correct backhand grip. The amount of rotation to the backhand grip is about one-sixteenth of a full turn of the handle. Try this: Spin the handle one full revolution within your hand. Then, twist the handle within your hand one-sixteenth of the full revolution that you performed in step one. The contrast in amounts of twist in these two steps should give you an idea of what a minor adjustment the grip change is. More on this soon.

The use of the off hand on the frame as described above is intended as a temporary racquet stabilizer and learning aid. Once you get the hang of the minor backhand grip adjustment, you will not use your left hand to facilitate the grip change. You will discard it, like you discarded training wheels after becoming confident at riding a bicycle.

Which direction to rotate when going from the forehand to the backhand grip is important. The rotation of the racquet handle is clockwise if you look at the handle from its butt end. Another way to explain the direction of rotation is that the V of your thumb and index finger falls farther to the left on the handle surface for the backhand grip. Still another way of describing the correct direction of rotation is to point out that the switch from the forehand to the backhand grip closes the racquet face—or angles the top of the frame slightly toward the floor.

How much to rotate gives novices more trouble than which direction. I already said the rotation should be about one-sixteenth of a full turn of the handle when changing from forehand to backhand grip. I used to tell my students to twist the handle an eighth of a turn, but 90 percent of them subsequently rotated too far. Now I tell them to twist it one-sixteenth of a turn and only about 50 percent of them rotate it too far. In other words, the general tendency

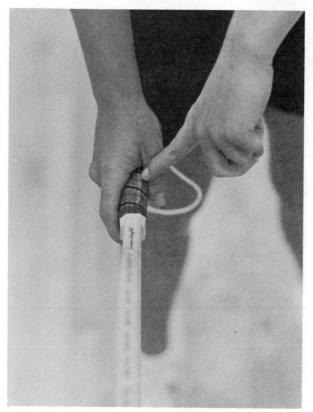

The correct backhand grip for the traditional two-grip system. The handle has been rotated about one-sixteenth of a turn from the forehand grip so that the thumb-index finger V in this photo lies over the left edge (where my finger points) of the top surface of the handle.

A close-up of the backhand grip showing the precise placement of the V over the left edge of the top surface. Note that you should wrap your thumb a little more tightly around the handle than the student in this photo is doing.

(which I'll expand on later) on the switch to the backhand grip is to overdo the turn. This causes the racquet face to close too much, which directs shots into the floor instead of straight at the front wall. If they call you "skipper" around your club and everyone plays to your backhand, check to see whether you adjust your grip too much.

Is this grip change still hazy? Let's approach it from a different angle. Reread step three in chapter 4, which explains that the V for the forehand grip falls on the middle of the topmost surface of the handle. Got it? Good, grab it, because now comes the shift of the V to the new point of reference for the backhand grip. The V should fall on the left edge of that topmost flat surface of the handle after you have made the one-sixteenth handle rotation to the backhand grip. Some instructors explain that the V for the backhand grip falls right over the bevel at which the top flat surface and its adjoining angled surface come together.

Try the change from the forehand to the backhand grip using each of the two points of reference that I just explained: the one-sixteenth turn and the V on the bevel. The result of either is the same—a more closed racquet face, which gives you flat, solid backhand shots.

I'm amazed at the number of players who can't figure out why the racquet won't rotate within their palms for even a sixteenth of a turn. These people try the handle twist with and without a glove, and still the racquet face won't close. They turn their wrists into painful contortions, then gaze down at their grip and scream because the V is exactly where it was for the forehand grip. Can you guess why? These players unconsciously continue to grasp the handle tightly while attempting to make the grip change. You must loosen your clench to allow the handle to rotate freely within your hand. This rotation is similar to an axle rotating within a sleeve, and no axle will turn if the sleeve is tight.

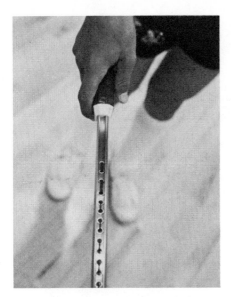

When the backhand grip is correct . . .

. . . the racquet face is square with or parallel to the front wall at the point of ball contact.

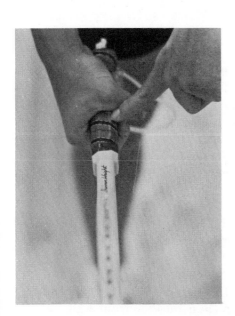

This is an incorrect grip for the backhand. Besides using an improper clenched fist in this photo, the V of my thumb-index finger is too much to the right (too close to the middle of the topmost surface, where the V normally lies for the forehand grip). Here I am pointing at the left edge of the top surface, over which the V should fall for the backhand. My improper grip here . . .

. . . causes the racquet face to slant upward (open) on backhand hits. This directs shots too high into the front wall (or ceiling) and gives backhand shots excess backspin slice.

This is another incorrect backhand grip, in which there has been an excessive shift from the forehand to the backhand grip. The V in this photo is way past the left edge of the top surface (my finger is pointing at this edge). This improper grip . . .

. . . causes the racquet face to slant down (closed) on the backhand stroke. The predictable result is consistent skip balls that typically have excess top spin.

Does one-sixteenth of a turn on the grip change seem so minute as to be inconsequential? I assure you that this small rotation has a dramatic effect on the outcome of your shots. Convince yourself of this right now by holding your racquet with the proper forehand grip. Now switch to the backhand grip while watching the head of the racquet. Not such a minor change way up there, is it? Your sixteenth of a turn at the handle closes the face about twenty degrees. This means that when you take a proper backhand swing and hit the ball in the ideal backhand contact area the strung racquet face will be parallel to the front wall. This translates into flatter, more solid, and harder hits—with no pesky bottom or top spin to dampen your backhand power.

In the one-grip system, the same grasp is used for the forehand and the backhand stroke. The grip is a compromise. Your thumb-index finger V should fall approximately over the area between the two arrows labeled "middle of top surface" and "upper left edge."

ONE-GRIP SYSTEM

Now let's look at the one-grip system. The grasps for the backhand and the forehand are the same with the one-grip method. That does *not* mean that you should use the traditional forehand grip (from the two-grip system) for your backhand strokes, nor should you use the traditional backhand grip (from the two-grip system) for your forehand strokes. Instead, the one-grip system is a *compromise* between the traditional forehand grip and the traditional backhand grip. The thumb-index finger V for the one-grip system should fall between the two previously described spots on the handle for the traditional forehand and backhand grips. That

is, the V for the one-grip system should rest about midway between the center and the left edge of the uppermost handle surface.

The obvious advantage of this compromise on the one-grip method is a faster reaction time on hard shots taken near the front wall. You won't get caught having to hit the ball while in the middle of the grip switch. The possible disadvantage of the one-grip method—especially among inexperienced players—is that despite the compromise between the two traditional grips, the racquet is still slightly open-faced on the backhand stroke. Unless some adjustment in the swinging arm or the depth of contact is made, this could result in backhand slices and too-high shots into the front wall.

Go ahead and give the one-grip technique a try. If it feels comfortable and your shots are right on, stick with it. Just remember that the one-grip method is a compromise—it is part traditional forehand and part traditional backhand. Many court newcomers make the mistake of grabbing their first racquet with the proper traditional forehand grip. It feels dandy, and they maintain this forehand grip for both strokes. Wrong! Typically, these greenhorn players eventually develop satisfactory forehands but lamentable backhands. Worse, the latter doesn't improve, no matter how long and hard they practice. The problem is the grip. I'll spell it out one more time: The racquet face angles improperly upward when you use a traditional forehand grip to swat a backhand shot. This open face directs shots higher than intended. Backhand kills become unintentional passes, intended passes come off the back wall for setups, and ceiling shots strike the ceiling too far back from the front wall. In addition to all this misdirection, a forehand grip causes backhand shots to come off the racquet strings with excess backspin and less power.

COMMON ERRORS

1. The most common error on the backhand grip (with the two-grip system) is neglecting to switch from the forehand grip when hitting backhand shots. Again, you can diagnose this problem yourself if you are aware that your backhand hits are not solid. They slice off the racquet strings with less zip and hit too high on the front wall.

2. I alluded earlier to this common error when detailing how much to switch the grip from forehand to backhand (with the two-grip method). Many players get overzealous at the prospect of a grip change that might improve their miserable backhand, and they change the grip too much.

Common error number one is using a forehand grip for backhand strokes. The grip shown here is okay for forehands but will hit backhands with an open-faced racquet.

Common error number 2. The incorrect grip pictured here will invariably angle shots into the floor because the face of the racquet is closed too much on backhand swings. The thumb-index finger V falls too far to the left of the left edge of the topmost surface.

Rotating the handle within your hand more than one-sixteenth of a turn when going from forehand to backhand closes the racquet face too much. Consequently, a normal swing will direct the ball too low for skips instead of front wall roll-offs. Another symptom of an exaggerated grip change is backhand shots that consistently have excess top spin. Check the V of your thumb and index finger on your backhand grip. If it falls to the left of the left edge of the uppermost handle surface, you have gone overboard on the grip change.

3. The most common error (with the one-grip system) is failing to realize that the one-grip is a compromise between the traditional forehand and backhand grips. Do not use the traditional forehand grip from the two-grip system to hit your backhands.

4. The infamous "thumb ball" is an interesting problem with the backhand grip that deserves special attention as a common error. Many novices misplace their thumbs when gripping for the backhand stroke. They bring their thumb over the racquet handle and toward the index finger so that it rests on the grip parallel to the length of the handle. That is, instead of wrapping around the handle, the thumb incorrectly lies along either the top flat surface or the left flat surface of the handle.

This thumb misplacement is said to hit thumb balls, in which the racquet and hitting arm are contorted weirdly in search of flat, solid backhand hits. This poses two problems (besides the fact that your backhand looks absolutely spastic): First, you lose a good deal of power. The hardest-hit thumb ball is a rubber turtle compared to a well-hit backhand using the correct grip. Second, you are likely to sprain your thumb.

Remember, your thumb should wrap around the handle in the opposite direction of the gripping fingers. It should come to rest somewhere between the index and middle fingers. More precisely, the flat of your thumb (the part they fingerprint) should rest approximately against the side of your middle finger (right against the side callus where a pencil rests when you write).

5. This and the remainder of the common errors on the backhand grip are the same as the last three errors listed in chapter 4 for the forehand grip. Therefore, I'll give only brief reviews of each of those problem areas. Refer to

An interesting variation of the misplaced thumb grip is this more frequently seen abortive grip. It precipitates the backhand "thumb ball." Here the thumb lies parallel along the back surface (rather than the top surface, as in the previous photo) of the handle. The thumb in this position can only push the ball on backhand strokes.

Common error number 4 is the misplaced thumb. The thumb should wrap around the grip rather than rest parallel to, and on the top surface of, the handle. This grip is practically powerless.

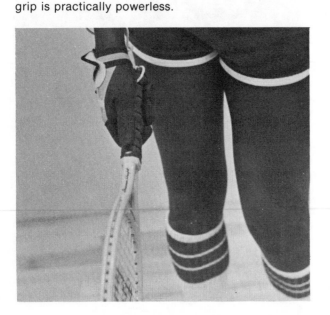

the common errors for the forehand grip if you wish further information.

Backhand grip error number five is using a fist grip. This incorrect technique is much less prevalent with the backhand than with the forehand.

6. Choking up too high on the racquet handle. Again, women are more prone to this than men.

7. Grasping the racquet too low on the handle. Court lads are more often guilty of this than court lasses.

Though the backhand grip (two-grip system) is just the forehand grip with a little twist, that tiny rotation is fraught with potential error. Get it right before proceeding to the backhand stroke.

Common error number 6 is the choke. Choking up too high on the handle is common among novice backhand grippers. Remember that the butt-of-racquet should go approximately against the heel-of-hand.

Common error number 5 is the fist grip. This is as improper on the backhand as it is the forehand. Correct the fist by spacing your index and middle fingers slightly apart.

Common error number 7. Holding the racquet too low on the handle is less frequently seen on the backhand than the forehand. Still, check to see that the little finger of your own hand is on at least the butt of the handle, rather than dangling worthlessly in the air.

You don't hammer a nail, chop wood, throw baseballs, or even swat flies with your backhand. Life really is prejudiced against the racquetball backhand stroke. It's no wonder your backhand is weaker than your forehand. But, fortunately, this can be cured. (Leach)

7
Backhand Stroke

INTRODUCTION TO BACKHAND

The major nemesis of many players on the court is not their opponent but their own backhand. Does this describe you? If so, it's probably because you haven't had many occasions during your life to use a motion even remotely resembling the backhand swing. You don't hammer a nail, chop wood, throw baseballs, swat flies, or even slap faces with your backhand. Life really is prejudiced against the racquetball backhand stroke. It's no wonder your backhand is weaker than your forehand, but we'll cure that with the instruction in this chapter.

No doubt, you have heard that the backhand is a potentially stronger stroke than the forehand. I concur, at least from the standpoint of

power. The curious anatomical arrangement of the human body puts the hitting arm on the rear shoulder (nearer the back wall) when you hit a forehand. On the other hand, it's on the lead shoulder (nearer the front wall) when you hit a backhand. Think about the ramifications of this. It means that forehands require more of a push across the body, but backhands require a sort of pull across the body.

If you dig this theoretical stuff but my explanation is still a little hazy, consider the analogy of the right-handed baseball batter. Both hands are on the bat when he swings at a ball. His right hand basically pushes the bat and his left hand pulls the bat across his body. Ergo, when the baseballer hits a home run, his right hand swings a forehand and his left hand swings a backhand—simultaneously! The important point in this analogy is that the backhand pull contributes *more* than the forehand push to generate stroke power for that home run.

Similarly, the backhand is the more powerful stroke in racquetball. But, you have to pull the hitting implement properly across your body to crack a home run or a backhand kill shot. The backhand model stroke I'm about to describe gives the stroke that is universally correct for the average player. As I explained in introducing chapter 5, you should use the model stroke as the basis for learning the backhand, but don't be afraid to make slight modifications to fit your personal physiotype and game style.

The backhand stroke and its add-ons are very similar to the forehand stroke and its add-ons. Therefore, if you followed and practiced the forehand add-on explanation, the backhand add-on game should be fast, fun, and easy. Remember that the add-on concept starts with the most basic movement or link and adds another movement-link and another, until the movements link up to form a chain that is called your backhand stroke. Since the backhand chain so closely resembles that of the forehand, I shall be much briefer in describing the following add-ons. The step numbers below are the same as in the forehand chapter, so if a particular add-on here seems too sketchy, refer to the same forehand step in chapter 5 for further explanation.

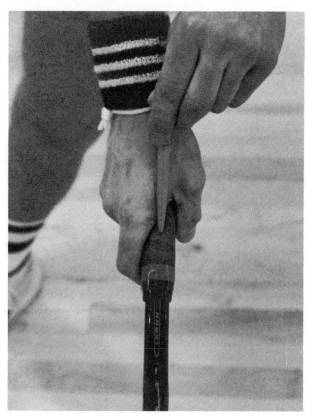

Add-on 1.

The starting stance for the series of backhand add-ons is approximately on the short line facing the left sidewall. Your feet should be nearly parallel to each other and pointing at that sidewall. As you get more experienced and start hitting the ball harder, you may move this starting station deeper in the court.

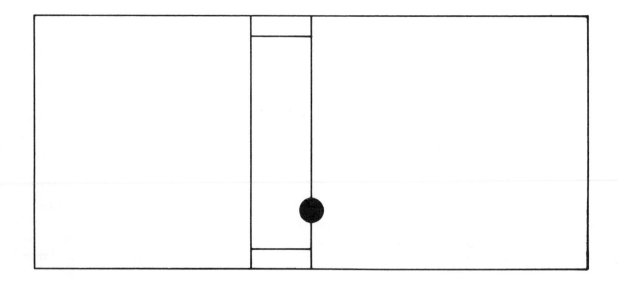

Add-on 2.

Add-on 3.

BACKHAND ADD-ONS

1. Grip your racquet with the proper backhand grip.

2. Stand on the court as you did for the forehand, except face the left sidewall on the short line—about an arm-and-a-racquet's length from that sidewall. Your feet should be comfortably apart, parallel and pointing at the left sidewall.

3. Close your backhand stance by sliding your right foot about two feet toward the left sidewall. Vary this closing distance a few inches more or less, depending on your height and build. Practice stepping into the closed stance about twenty times.

4. Extend your arm in front of the belt buckle of your gym shorts so that the racquet

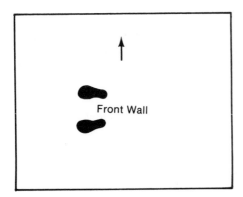

This is the incorrect open stance for the backhand. It has your lead (right) foot no closer to the left sidewall than your rear (left) foot. On the other hand . . .

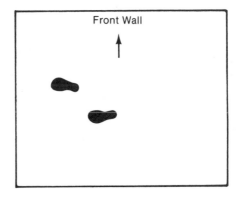

. . . the correct closed stance during backhand contact has your lead foot about two feet closer to the left sidewall than your rear foot.

Add-on 4.

points at the sidewall. Cock your wrist for the backhand. Here is the first major deviation from the forehand add-on, so let's take a closer look at the backhand wrist cock.

5. If you have combined add-ons one through four, you are now in a closed stance with your arm straight out toward the left wall and with your wrist flexed back and up, holding the racquet in the backhand cocked position. Don't change anything in this step, except for a simple add-on: take your racquet back one foot for a very short backswing. This backswing should be flat and level. Got it? Careful, maintain the wrist cock and don't start the backswing more than a foot back. No forward swing yet; just take the racquet back. Repeat about twenty times.

6. Let's now add the familiar wrist flick, without a ball. This two-foot flick-swing (one foot of backswing and one foot of follow-through) must be about knee-high. Keep it level and parallel to the floor. What we have is an

The backhand wrist cock is a flexing back and up of the wrist. However, the more important part of this, which contributes more to the subsequent wrist snap at ball contact, is the flexing back. To flex your wrist back into the cock position (without the racquet), extend your arm and hand with fingers pointing straight ahead.

Flex your wrist at the joint so that your fingers point to the left. This is the back flexion for the backhand cock. Also, remember that you should tilt your wrist up a little (angle your fingers upward slightly). Now add a racquet to your hand to get a feel for the backhand wrist cock without a backswing. Then . . .

. . . add the upward tilt of the wrist and the backswing. This photo shows my backhand wrist cock just as I'm bringing the racquet down from the top of the backswing. Cocking your wrist back and up is like cocking a gun—it readies your weapon for shooting.

Add-on 5. Take the racquet into a one-foot backswing with your wrist still cocked.

A poll taken among the pro players a few years ago proclaimed Marty Hogan's backhand as the best in the game's history. Since that time, Hogan's backhand has gotten stronger! A common question in clinics is what to do with the nonhitting arm during the swing. Just let it hang out of your armpit and flow naturally with the movement of the upper body. Or, in this photo, use it to locate the side of the court fishbowl. (Capiel)

Add-on 6.

abbreviated stroke with a gentle (for now) wrist snap at midswing, or the point of imaginary ball contact.

7. This is the ball add-on. Bounce the ball on the floor, as you did on the forehand, at a spot about one foot behind (toward the back wall) and two feet out (toward the left sidewall) from your right lead foot. The ball should rebound from the floor and peak about knee-high. Catch it just after it starts to descend from its zenith. Repeat until your bounces and catches are consistent. Try this step at least twenty times.

8. Now combine steps six and seven. Drop and hit the ball in the proper contact zone just after it peaks at knee height. Use only a one-foot backswing and a one-foot follow-through to wrist-flick the ball straight into the front wall. The proper contact zone for the backhand has three dimensions: (1) distance from body, (2) depth (farther forward or farther back toward the back wall), and (3) height.

Remember that for now there is no step or body rotation before the swing, and the short

This sequence portrays all the add-ons up to and including add-on 6. You only get a two-foot stroke up to this point. This includes a cocked one-foot backswing *(top)*, the short downswing *(above)*, which is horizontal or approximately parallel with the floor, a wrist flick-snap *(opposite top)* at the potential point of ball contact, and a one-foot follow-through *(opposite center)*, which is also approximately parallel with the floor *(opposite bottom)*. Don't worry if your abbreviated stroke here feels a bit strange. There are ten more add-ons to smooth things out.

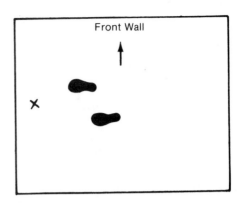

The spot (X) on the floor where you bounce the ball for the drop-and-hit drills is about a foot behind and two feet out from your lead foot.

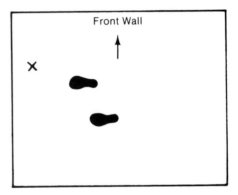

If you bounce and contact the ball too far forward, you'll get less steam on the shot and will consistently pull the ball crosscourt.

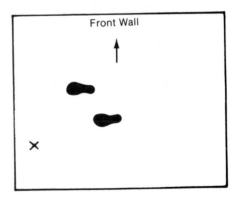

If you bounce and contact the ball too deep in your stance, your wrist probably won't have the time or room to snap before ball contact. This greatly decreases power and causes most shots to glance into the left sidewall.

Add-on 7.

Add-on 8.

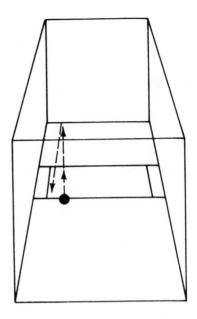

Aim your backhand shots in these add-ons straight into the front wall at an area that is knee- to waist-high and two or three feet from the left sidewall. Catch the rebound. Repeat.

In this photo, I'm about to hit the ball: (1) comfortably out from my body without reaching or jamming my swing, (2) just behind my lead foot after I've stepped into the stroke, and (3) the ball is descending and will be just below my knees when it meets my racquet.

stroke is flat and parallel to the floor. Place an imaginary table under the path of your racquet and another above that path. These will flatten out your swing. Then put a brick wall a foot back from the point of ball contact, and another one foot ahead of that point of contact. These will prevent you from exceeding the two-foot swing with your backswing or follow-through.

Direct your shots for this step directly into the front wall, up and down the backhand line. Catch the ball when it comes to you from the front wall. Repeat twenty times, or until the movement becomes smooth and consistent.

9. This step adds on two more horizontal feet of level stroke. You now get to take a two-foot backswing and a two-foot follow-through. In other words, the mental tables remain stationary, but the brick walls are demolished and reconstructed parallel and four feet apart. This greater leeway allows you a longer, more powerful swing and a better wrist snap at midpoint in the stroke. Repeat this step twenty or so times.

10. Now add even more stroke power with an additional one foot of backswing and one foot of follow-through. Hit and retrieve a shot with this level six-foot swing, catch the ball, then rehit and retrieve again, about twenty times.

11. Now is the time for maximum backswing and follow-through. The ready position for this step is the closed stance with your racquet cocked in your maximum backswing. Maximum is as deep as feels comfortable. Just remember that the swing is still knee-high and fairly level throughout the maximally comfortable follow-through.

Got it? Now drop and hit the ball, making contact as usual in the proper contact zone just below your knees. There goes the ball—straight and hard into the front wall. Here it comes back—straight and hard at you. Catch and do it again and again.

12. Here's where we make the backswing less awkward with a simple add-on. Start with the racquet drawn back into your maximum

Bouncing the ball for backhand drop-and-hits sometimes confuses beginning players. There are two methods: (1) You can have your left arm over your right when you drop the ball . . .

. . . or, (2) you can bounce with your left arm under your right. Either way is okay, though you'll probably find the second method easier when you start taking a deeper and higher backswing.

Add-on 9. The wrist flick-stroke in this step starts with a two-foot backswing with the wrist cocked. Your swing should be fairly horizontal, including only a two-foot follow-through.

Add-on 10. Drop and hit the ball using a three-foot backswing and a three-foot follow-through. Is there a noticeable increase of power compared to the previous two-foot backswing stroke?

This photo sequence illustrates add-on 10, in which you use a six-foot stroke *(below left)* to hit the ball.

Note that I am starting with my racquet down near the forthcoming point of contact *(below center)*, and as the ball bounces I'll draw it back. You may use this method, or use the regular technique of starting with your racquet in the backswing cocked position before dropping the ball. Bounce the ball, and . . .

Add-on 11.

Add-on 12.

. . . draw your racquet to a three-foot flat backswing *(opposite right)*.

Begin your downswing as the ball peaks at knee height *(below left)*. This means that . . .

. . . you hit the ball just after it peaks—just below your knees *(below center)*. Then . . .

. . . for now, your follow-through should be only about three feet. Try to keep it flat—nearly parallel to the floor *(below right)*.

The Marty Hogan backhand wrist cock. Do you see that his wrist flexes both up and back? If you took the racquet out of his hand, the cock back means a flexion of the wrist, as though your fingers are trying to touch the skin wrinkles over which you take a pulse, and the cock up means a flexion upward. (Bledsoe)

backswing position as in the previous step. The face of the racquet should lie in a plane approximately parallel to your shoulders. Now crook your elbow ninety degrees. As with the forehand elbow crook, the tricep-bicep portion of your upper arm should be about parallel with the floor, and your forearm should point up at the ceiling.

Understand that we have removed the upper imaginary table boundary for this and the ensuing steps, but the lower table remains to keep your stroke flat rather than underhanded. Drop the ball, swing, and hit as before. Repeat until you've done it enough times.

13. This step is just a *step*—into the ball. Up to now, you have not taken a stride into your swings, but instead have started out in the closed stance—as if you had already stepped into the shot. But now I want you to begin in an open stance, with feet parallel to each other and equidistant from the sidewall. (This is the same starting stance as for the first step in this series of backhand add-ons.) Ready? Without the ball, step from an open into a closed stance by bringing your right foot a couple of feet closer to the left sidewall. That's all; no swing. Repeat twenty times, or until the movement becomes subconscious.

Add-on 13. Start in an open stance and . . .

. . . step into a closed stance.

14. Now you are going to step into, and swing at, an imaginary ball. Stride into a closed stance with your lead foot as in the previous step, then swing at air. Pretend that you are blasting the ball low and straight into the front wall. Stand back up to admire your shot. Do it again and again until you have put away a couple dozen imaginary kill shots.

15. Back to reality. This add-on adds the ball to the previous step. Do it.

Keep in mind that this is a run-on of add-ons. It should be a smooth sequence of continuous motion, rather than a staccato connection of separate movements. If your stroke is jerky at first, don't fret. Each ensuing practice session will be like speeding up the individual frames of a motion picture, until they blend into a continuous show. Find out for yourself by practicing this step until you're satisfied.

16. This final step provides the last link in the chain that produces the model backhand stroke. Let's get some body rotation into your swing. Many greenhorn racquetballers resemble ar-

Add-on 14.

In this photo, Ernie Charfauros waits for the ball to rebound off the back wall. Ernie's backswing is cocked and flat (perhaps a tad low), his shoulders are turned away from the front wall in the body coiled backswing position, and his feet are in a closed stance. When the ball comes off the back wall, this will be a rolloff shot in the left front corner. It should hit the front wall first so it will carry away from the covering opponent. (Charfauros)

Add-on 14 is just a step into an imaginary ball. Begin with an open stance *(left)* and step into the backhand closed stance *(right)*. During play, step into the closed stance on forehands and backhands whenever there is ample time on the setup. Be cautioned, however, that this fast-moving game doesn't offer ample time on every setup during the rally, which means that you will be forced now and then to hit from an open stance.

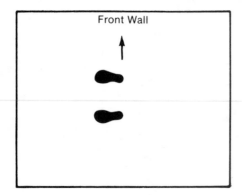

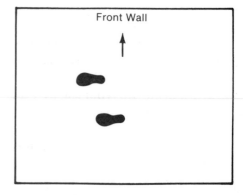

Add-on 15. Start in an open stance and bounce the ball so it will peak at knee height.

Step into a closed stance as the ball hits the floor.

Start your downswing as your lead foot hits the floor, then start your wrist snap just before ball contact.

Hit the ball after it peaks in your contact zone. Use as little body rotation as possible in this step—that comes in the next and final add-on.

Add-on 16. Coil your hips and shoulders on the backswing, then . . .

. . . uncoil during the downswing and follow-through. The coil-uncoil adds body rotation to your swing, which greatly boosts stroke power.

thritic rock-and-roll dancers in that they fail to shake their hips. You have to use your hips in racquetball to get the weight transfer that engenders maximum stroke power. I'm talking about the same coil-step-uncoil sequence discussed for the forehand in chapter 5. Reread that section now if you don't recall the rationale behind weight transfer and getting your body into the ball.

Let's add body rotation to your backhand: Start with the same cocked backswing as in the preceding two steps, but now rotate your body a little toward the left rear court corner—just a little bit of body coil for now. Then drop the ball in preparation for the swing. Your body may have a tendency to turn even more toward the left rear corner just after the ball hits the floor. Let it, because this additional coil means more power. Just after the ball hits the floor,

Body rotation—the coil on the backswing. Body rotation is especially important in the generation of power on the backhand stroke.

If you've ever thrown a frisbee, your body is already programmed for body rotation, backswing, step forward, wrist snap, and weight transfer on the backhand stroke. The two body motions are remarkably similar. Having trouble generating power on your backhand swings? Pretend the racquet is a frisbee.

This is a photo sequence of add-on 16, with a lower limiting barrier to flatten out the swing. (You should use an imaginary barrier if you suspect your swing is too underhanded.) Note two important points in this series of pictures. First, the head of the racquet sweeps almost horizontally through the contact zone above the center of the box. Therefore, the racquet handle is fairly parallel to, rather than dipping toward, the floor. This flat swing assures side-to-side (horizontal) accuracy on the bottom board target area of the front wall.

The second important stroke pointer in this photo sequence concerns body rotation. You should coil your body on the backswing—rotate your hips and shoulders toward the back wall on the backswing. Then uncoil your body—thrust your hips and shoulders around toward the front wall—during the downswing.

In sum, a level swing through the contact zone gives accuracy. Good body rotation gives power. And aren't accuracy and power what the racquetball strokes are all about?

step into the closed stance. This step initiates the uncoil of your pelvis and shoulders. Twist them around forcefully. The downswing begins just after the pelvis and shoulders start to uncoil. You should be able to feel a forward shift of body weight from rear to front foot—and from your body to your racquet to the ball.

The resulting rubber-on-string is a smashing meeting. High-speed photography reveals that a powerful stroke generates such rapid racquet head speed that during string contact—the time between initial ball contact and eventual ball release—some very interesting things occur. The ball flattens on the strings as if suddenly deflated; the strings give, or bend back like a sheet of thin rubber paper; the entire racquet frame flexes backward from the throat; and the sides of the frame simultaneously collapse slightly around the ball.

Isn't that scenario remarkably similar to your backhand rips? If not, practice step sixteen some more.

The Model Backhand: Bounce the ball and . . .

. . . your body starts to coil toward the back wall, as . . .

. . . you draw your racquet back, body rotating more . . .

. . . until you reach the top of the backswing with your maximum body coil. Now . . .

. . . your step into the stroke initiates your downswing, . . .

. . . you contact the ball in the proper contact zone below your knees, and . . .

. . . your follow-through is fairly compact and level, ending with

. . . your hips open to the front wall. (Compare this photo sequence to the previous one of the frisbee throw. Specifically, look for these similarities: body coil, backswing, step forward, downswing, wrist snap, body uncoil, and weight transfer.)

SUMMARY OF ADD-ONS

1. Grip the racquet with the proper backhand grip.

2. Stand on the short line facing the left sidewall.

3. Close your stance.

4. Extend your racquet toward the sidewall and cock your wrist up and back.

5. Take a one-foot backswing, with the wrist still cocked. No swing yet.

6. Take a two-foot stroke with a wrist flick—without the ball.

7. Bounce the ball on the floor so that it peaks in the center of the proper contact zone. Catch the ball after it peaks.

8. Bounce and hit the ball with a two-foot wrist-flick stroke—one-foot backswing and one-foot follow-through.

9. Bounce and hit the ball with a two-foot backswing and a two-foot follow-through.

10. Bounce and hit the ball with a three-foot backswing and a three-foot follow-through.

11. Bounce and hit the ball with your maximally comfortable backswing and follow-through. The swing is level and about knee-high throughout.

12. Make the backswing more proper by crooking your elbow at ninety degrees, with your forearm pointing up at the ceiling.

13. Start with an open stance and then step into a closed stance, as though stepping into the ball. Do not swing yet.

14. Start with an open stance, step into a closed stance, and swing at an imaginary ball.

15. Step into and hit the ball.

16. Add body rotation to your swing by coiling your hips and shoulders on the backswing, uncoiling on the downswing.

It is sometimes difficult to differentiate between over-swinging and trying too hard, especially on the professional level. Symptoms of overswinging are muscle tetany and a tortured grimace on the face. Do you suspect you are overswinging on shots? Then try letting up on your swing effort just 10 percent, and evaluate the effect on your power and control. (Leach)

8
Stroke — Common Errors and Pointers

INTRODUCTION

The common errors for the forehand and backhand are generally the same. For example, the common error of an underhanded swing exists for both strokes. Moreover, if you are guilty of a particular error on your forehand, it is likely that you will commit the same mistake with your backhand. For example, if a player contacts the ball too high or swings too softly, she usually does so on both strokes.

Use this chapter as a checklist or test of your strokes. Ask yourself about each error, "Do I do this?" If the answer is yes, correct it. Such self-analysis works only if you are very objective. Give yourself a split personality if you have to, and pretend you are using the common error list to check someone else's stroke rather than your own.

If you discover that you are committing more than one of these errors, list your common errors and arrange the list starting with the easiest and moving to the most difficult to correct. Work on the first error on the list until you correct it, then practice to correct the next error. Continue in this manner until you've gone through the whole list and your stroke is model-perfect.

The following list of common errors is comprehensive and detailed. Many of the mistakes listed could be considered stroke pointers rather than errors. I say pointers because these paragraphs contain fresh material not presented in the previous chapters on the forehand and the backhand. A summary listing of the errors and pointers at the end of this chapter provides a quick common error (and stroke) review. Let's begin.

Improper grip. Have a qualified player evaluate your grip before you spend hundreds of hours practicing an incorrect technique.

Perhaps the most frequent grip mistake is holding the racquet with a forehand grip to hit backhand shots. This causes, as shown in this photo, the racquet face to slant up too much at ball contact.

Probably the second most common grip error is holding the racquet too high on the handle. This decreases leverage, which cuts down on your swing power. Choke up a little if you wish, but not this much.

COMMON ERRORS AND POINTERS

1. Improper Grip

This common stroke error starts way back with the grip. If your grip hasn't got it, neither will your stroke. Grip error usually leads to an altitude problem. Your shots (especially when your swing is rushed or in some other way stressed) will consistently either skip too low or fly too high at the front wall. If you are experiencing either of these symptoms, check the grip error sections at the ends of chapters 4 and 6 on the forehand and backhand grips.

2. Too Much Model

Some players see a sequence of stroke photos in an instructional book and immediately determine these to be unequivocal paragons for them to emulate. This leads to the mistake of using too much model and too little natural swing in the stroke. I don't expect or want you to replicate the pictures and descriptions of the model strokes in this book. Instead, mesh them with your natural swing, which is dictated by your physiotype, psychotype, etc. Develop a hybrid swing—part model and part natural—that is both comfortable and potent.

Too Much Model.

Backhand Run-around.

3. Backhand Run-around

This common error may help improve your forehand, but at the same time it retards your backhand development. The guilty party is usually the backhand-less player. This is the person who often doesn't even acknowledge the existene of a backhand stroke. When a ball comes to the left side of her body, she either runs around her backhand to hit a forehand, or she wheels and hits the ball with her forehand into the back wall, hoping it will rebound on the fly to the front wall for a legal return.

Of course, you may choose to live out the rest of your racquetball career as a strictly one-stroke player, and it is possible that you will

One form of guarding the backhand is by using the forehand ball-into-back-wall shot. In this, the player sees a ball coming to the backhand side and, instead of swinging a backhand, he or she wheels around . . .

. . . and hits the ball into the back wall with a forehand. The idea is that the ball will carry to the front wall on the fly. True, it often will—but the resulting setup off the front wall is invariably an absolute plum ball. You should instead try to return balls on the backhand side of your body with a backhand stroke. (Steppe)

enjoy yourself. But it is more likely that such a career will be somewhat short-lived because you'll quickly get discouraged at being stomped in games all the time. One-sided players are losers unless they select their opponents carefully.

This error of run-around is more prevalent among women than among men. Typically, the player is embarrassed at the prospect of displaying her impotent backhand. So she hides it behind a series of forehands. I encourage all closet backhanders to come out and unveil their backhands as soon as possible. Learn early in your court career to live with the temporary embarrassment, then work on backhand improvement.

I tell my closet one-stroke students that there are at least three ways to improve their backhands quickly:

1. Do just the opposite of what you are accustomed to doing. That is, get into the habit of running around your forehand to hit a back-

hand. For example, if the ball rebounds off the back wall for a setup in the middle of the court, position yourself so that the ball comes to the left side of your body. Note that running around the forehand to hit a backhand is a corrective technique, *not* a correct technique. After your backhand improves, it will no longer be necessary to run around either stroke.

2. Play the left or backhand side when you play doubles. Many pro players developed their backhands into formidable weapons only after playing a few months of doubles as the left-side player. (Incidentally, I do *not* recommend playing doubles when you are at the beginning or intermediate levels of play. It's downright dangerous. But if you must engage in this four-woman foolery, wear eyeguards and play the backhand side.)

3. Most important, your solo practice sessions should devote twice as much time to the backhand as to the forehand. This means that when you go through the drill regimen in chap-

Overswinging. Too many players think that harder is better. It is better only if you have the same control and aren't straining your arm.

Are you confusing stroke activity with stroke production? A helicopter windup and windmill follow-through don't necessarily signify efficiency or power. You simply may be overswinging.

ter 9, hit forty backhands if you hit twenty forehands for each drill. Practice your weaknesses, not your strengths.

4. Overswinging

One of the most common questions asked by beginning players concerns how hard to hit the ball. A general rule is that you should swing with about 80 percent of your maximum stroke power. Too many players think that harder is better—regarding how hard they swing their hitting arms. If you swing with an all-out 100-percent maximum flail, you lose accuracy and will soon strain your arm.

Do you suspect that you are overswinging? Try letting up on your stroke effort just 10 percent and see what happens to your power and control. If you gain a lot of accuracy at the expense of only a small loss of ball velocity, swinging a tad easier might be the answer to your stroke problems.

Shyness Syndrome. The shyness syndrome is usually an attitude problem—a lack of assertiveness or being afraid of the ball.

5. Shyness Syndrome

This common error is easy to define, diagnose, and correct. Your only problem might be that you are not objective enough to admit that you are plagued by the shyness syndrome in the first place.

The shyness syndrome is basically an attitude problem that affects mainly the female player who is relatively new to the sport. This woman is as timid as Caspar Milquetoast when it comes to belting the ball. Typically, she bends daintily at the knees when picking up the ball, she won't run hard after the ball because it might cause perspiration, and she administers love taps instead of kill shots. I'm not kidding and I'm not making fun. Too many lady newcomers are overly concerned about their femininity on the court.

Let me dispel the myth that you cannot be feminine and competitive at the same time. The women on the pro tour dress like ladies and act like ladies—they are ladies. But, they don't fear that walloping the rubber cover off the ball will sully their female visages. Racquetball is a power game, whatever the sex of the participants. Don't expect to play pattycake on the court and still have fun or win. Yep, it's a kick to blast the ball—and it's terrific fun to win in the process.

The solution to the shy syndrome? Well, your gut reaction to the solution I use in clinics, which I'm about to describe, might be one of mild disgust, but try it and see if it doesn't cure your timidity about really working on your strokes. I sometimes tell shy clinic swingers to pretend that the ball is the head of a disliked person. An old boyfriend they used to date works just fine as a target cranium. "Now," I tell them, "clobber that guy's head into the front wall!" It works every time.

The shyness syndrome is a mental one. Cure it with a good dose of adrenalin.

6. Underswinging

The shyness syndrome is closely related to this common error, but the two are nonetheless separate problems that have different solutions. Many women are as competitive as wildcats and think that sweat is celestial, but they swing like pussycats. This is clearly not a case of the shyness syndrome, but is simply a problem of underswinging.

Often players incorrectly reason that the softer they swing, the more control they have. They figure they can pinpoint their shots better when they gently lay, rather than smash, the ball into the front corner. This is dead wrong.

The harder you swing—up to about a firm 80 percent of maximum power—the *more* control you have. This may not seem logical at first, but I know it is true both from teaching others and from personal experience.

I believe I can explain this ostensible paradox to convince all doubting soft strokers. The slower your stroke, the jerkier your stroke. When you slow down the stroke motion, the chain of movement add-ons goes from smooth to staccato. This is like slowing down a movie of a player hitting the racquetball. The slower the movie rolls, the more uneven and unnatural the swing looks. Speed up the movie, and the motion blends into a continuous, natural stroke.

Let's go from the movies to bicycles for further support of my point. Remember the first time you got on a bicycle? You probably hopped on, pedaled tentatively a few times, and zig-zagged slowly down the sidewalk. As you became more experienced, you pedaled faster and the bike miraculously became better balanced. You went in a straight line down the sidewalk. Now do you agree with my analogy? It is valid, especially when you consider that even the experienced bicyclist who slows down, and slows down more, will soon be going so slowly that his rhythm and balance will be thrown out of kilter. It's zigzag time again.

There are two ways to determine whether you are underswinging. First, you can ask somebody or a bunch of somebodies if they think you swing too softly. Second, you can test yourself. Do this: Drop and hit a normal forehand or backhand (whichever stroke you suspect you may be underswinging on) straight into the front wall. Repeat this drop-and-hit four or five times, or until you get a feel for that stroke's

Underswinging. Underswinging is not always due to being shy. Some players just think the racquetball strokes are supposed to be smooth and flowing rather than a controlled explosion.

If you're smiling, you're probably underswinging.

power and accuracy. Now repeat that step, but hit four or five shots with your normal stroke, *plus* 10 percent swing power. In other words, concentrate on bringing the racquet around just a bit harder. If after you complete this step you feel like you are already overswinging—using more swing strength than feels natural and comfortable—then quit right there. The added 10 percent is enough. But, if you are not yet overhitting and you are still dissatisfied with your power and accuracy, hit four or five more shots with an *additional* 10 percent of power. Not overswinging yet? Then keep adding on 10-percent increments in stroke power until you come up with the correct amount of oomph in your swing.

I have stated that about 80 percent of your all-out oomph is about right, but this will vary slightly from player to player. The idea is to experiment with gradual increases of effort until you reach the comfortable maximum swing that provides the most satisfactory mix of power and control. Remember, the racquetball stroke is similar to a karate punch—firm and focused but not wild and all-out.

A side note here: Swinging harder—up to your comfortable maximum—not only scores winners through increased shot accuracy, it also fetches points in a subtler way. The harder you swing, the harder the ball goes. The faster the ball goes, the less time your opponent has to react to your mis-hit shots. The opposite holds, too. The softer you hit the ball, the more time your rival has to cover your mis-hit shots. And believe me, we're all going to have mis-hits.

Let's illustrate this with a specific example. I hit the ball harder than most of the other women on the pro tour. This means that when one of my kill shots goes too high into the front wall, it nonetheless caroms back so fast that my opponent is often jammed, or rushed, on her return. I still get the point by virtue of sheer ball velocity. You can just as easily see that my slower-hitting opponent loses a big edge on *her* mis-hit kill attempts. Her balls rebound off the front wall like daisies floating in the wind, and I have time to yawn, wave to the crowd, and still rekill the return.

I'll conclude this underswinging common error with a related two-point hypothesis: (1) If all of the skills—control, stamina, savvy, etc.—of two players in a racquetball game are equivalent with the singular exception of power, the harder-hitting player will win every time. (2) The good power player who has average control will beat the good control player who has average power every time.

In sum, accuracy hurts, but speed kills the opponent. Don't tap, push, guide, or otherwise underswing at the ball. Hit it hard.

7. Push Stroke

Pushing the ball with your racquet may be a cause of underswinging, but I classify it here as a separate error because it is a specific problem for many female players. Racquetball is a wristy sport. If you fail to acknowledge this by maintaining a stiff wrist throughout the swing, you end up hitting with the feeble push stroke.

Remember, the wrist must cock on the backswing and snap at ball contact. You should hear a brisk swish of air when your wrist snaps the racquet during a swing at an imaginary ball.

Push Stroke. Pushing, rather than swinging at the ball with a forceful wrist snap at ball contact, is a common error prevalent among novice female players.

This swish is from the strings whipping through the air when the racquet head moves faster—which is during the wrist pop at the potential point of contact. If you're not swishing, you're not snapping.

The solution to the push? Be cognizant of the wrist cock at the top of the backswing. Then consciously flex the wrist quickly at midswing. It's like slapping someone across the face, only with a racquet in your palm. Try the wrist snap at first without a racquet. The flip-flop movement is like fanning. Now grab the racquet and fan more air. If you now think you've got the snap of it, ask a buddy if she thinks you're using enough wrist flick on your swing. If she says no, review the wrist-flick add-on steps in the stroke chapters.

8. No Body

Do you swing mainly with your arm, without using the power of the rest of your body? Does the force of gravity pull your kill shots down

No Body.

This sequence shows an exaggerated lack of body rotation on the forehand stroke. The hips and shoulders aren't turned enough toward the right rear corner on the backswing, and . . .

. . . they don't open up enough during the **downswing** and **follow-through**. No power here.

This sequence shows an exaggerated lack of body rotation on the backhand stroke. There is no hip or shoulder coil toward the left rear corner on the backswing.

Only the arm swings on the downswing, and . . .

. . . the body stays square to the sidewall rather than more properly opening to face the front wall. Again, no power here.

The backhand body rotation is very similar to throwing a frisbee. There is similar turning of the hips and shoulders on the windup/backswing, . . .

. . . similar downswings, where the hips and shoulders rotate forcefully around . . .

. . . and similar follow-throughs in which the front of the body opens up to the front wall.

Remember that body coil (on the backswing) plus body uncoil (on the downswing and follow-through) equals stroke power. Try adding more body rotation to your stroke in progressive 10-percent increments: (1) Hit shots with your normal stroke. (2) Add 10 percent body rotation and compare your power. (3) Add 10 percent more rotation and compare. (4) Continue adding 10-percent power increments until you attain a comfortable amount of body coil-uncoil, which produces satisfactory power without sacrificing accuracy.

into the floor more than the force of your swing propels the ball horizontally toward the front wall? Or, is your swing just as wristy and energetic as the next player's, but her strokes hit with a bang and yours with a whimper? It may be, as I mentioned in the final add-on in the forehand stroke chapter, that you never learned to shake your hips and roll your shoulders on the dance floor. It's time to get your body into the stroke.

Reread that final step sixteen in chapter 5 if you are unsure about getting enough body into the ball. Remember that coil plus uncoil equals power. Try this: (1) Hit four or five shots into the front wall with your regular stroke. Note the feel of the amount of power your stroke generates. (2) Add about 10 percent body rotation on

the backswing to your regular stroke. Again, note the resulting power. (3) Add 10 percent more body coil on the backswing—and continue to increase the hip and shoulder rotation by 10-percent increments until you come up with a comfortable amount of body coil that produces satisfactory power.

9. Step-less Swing

Think now—do you step into the ball when you swing? If you do, your body weight properly transfers from rear foot during the backswing to front foot during the follow-through, and you get more oomph out of your stroke. But if you don't step forward into the shot, you are squandering a lot of potential power. That's

Step-less Swing.

the front wall. Subsequently, they have to lean backward during the swing to allow the ball to drop to knee height. The cure is to set up deeper on the ball as it comes at you. Then you can stride forward without stepping past the ball as it drops into the proper contact zone—knee-high.

The inexperienced racquetballer tends to charge the ball as it rebounds off the front wall. She overruns the sphere and ends up hitting it with a step-less swing while falling backward. Overrunning the setup also leads to these common symptoms: too-high ball contact, a rushed swing, weight still on the rear foot during the follow-through, and a subsequent aborted stroke.

Here's a gimmick to cure ball rushing. As the ball rebounds off the front wall and you see that you'll have plenty of time to set up on the shot, back up a couple of steps. Then get ready with your backswing and wait. Now, as the ball takes its floor bounce and descends, step forward to hit as it enters your contact zone. Did you still contact the ball too high that time? Then, on the next setup, back up more steps so that the sphere has the opportunity to descend to knee height before you swing.

If you must lean one way or another on your swing, lean forward instead of backward. This way, though the stroke may not be textbook-correct, at least your body weight moves forward and transfers from your racquet to the ball in terms of greater shot velocity.

very bad news in this power game. You'll also know you are using an incorrect step-less swing if during the follow-through you sense that your body weight rests on your rear foot, or if you fall backward while you swing.

The problem here can be traced to *setting up* on the shot. Many women set up too close to

A step-less swing typically goes hand-in-hand with an open stance. Here the young lady sets up in an open stance, and . . .

. . . not only does she fail to step into a closed stance, but she fails to step into the ball at all.

Many players set up on the ball too near the front wall.

10. Slow Setup

This common error causes some of the previous ones. The error lies in not setting up quickly enough on a shot during the rally. Is your swing rushed, or do you contact the ball too late or too deep? Your timing or your footwork is off. Cure either by setting up more quickly. By this I mean that you must get your racquet back and get your tennis shoes moving the instant you know where the ball is going.

Let's look at setting up in more detail. Your initial move after deciding whether the ball is coming to your forehand or your backhand should be to assume a ready-and-waiting position. If the ball is coming to your forehand, then turn to face the right sidewall; if it is headed at your backhand, then face the left sidewall. Now, move to the correct position on the court to await the ball's drop into your contact zone. As you move after the ball, you should take your racquet up into the cocked backswing position to ensure stroke readiness. (What good is exemplary footwork if your gun

In doubles play the racquetball darts around the court so fast that it often forces the players into unorthodox positions when returning shots, such as in this photo of Sheryl Ambler smashing a forehand in a pro doubles match. (Oram)

Slow Setup. Setting up too slowly on shots is almost always due to lazy footwork. If you have guilty feet, get them moving.

You must move quickly when setting up on shots, or else you'll likely end up in some strange stances about the time the ball descends to knee height and is ready to be hit.

isn't cocked when it's time to shoot?) Now step into the shot as the ball descends to knee height. Then swing away.

The important point here is that all the setting up described in the preceding paragraph must be done rapidly—in a second or less after you determine where in the court the ball will descend to knee height. Thus, there are two important steps to setting up: (1) Knowing where on the court you will be hitting the shot (where the ball will descend to knee height), and (2) getting quickly to that area with your racquet in the backswing ready position.

That's the theoretical solution, at least. It will help your slow setup woes but, in some cases, it may not cure them. I remarked earlier that setting up is a matter of timing. Well, learning timing takes time. Don't think that, just because you swing late on every shot, you have glue on your feet, cement in your bottom, and mush in your head. Poor setting up is instead often due to a lack of on-the-job training. Don't worry. Experience will expand time so that as you become more proficient, you will have plenty of time to set up on shots. Fortunately, you can catalyze the acquisition of experience and setup time with big doses of solo and game practice.

Think about your strokes. Do you usually end up following through with your body weight resting on your rear foot? Do you finish the swing while leaning backward? This is called setting up slowly. Remedy it by getting your tennis shoes moving the instant you know where the ball is going off the front wall.

Setting Up On the Ball. Your initial move after deciding whether the ball is coming to your forehand or backhand should be to assume a ready-and-waiting position. If the ball is coming to your forehand, then turn to

(caption continued on next page)

face the right sidewall. If it is headed at your back-hand, then face the left sidewall. Then move to the correct position on the court to await the ball's drop into your contact zone.

Besides expanding time, experience also contracts the court. I'm not kidding. Remember how huge the court seemed the first time you toddled through the door? Your eyeballs were as big as racquetballs as you pondered the hardwood vastness. You looked straight ahead and there on the horizon was the front wall. Less distant, yet still appearing about a day's journey from each other, were the sidewalls. Then you looked up and blinked in awe at the number and brightness of all the suns up there in that flat white sky. Indeed, on your first outing the racquetball court seemed like a large, ominous, square world. But now you're experienced—a callused veteran. The court has shrunk. The front wall is only a few steps from the back, and the sidewalls are just a few racquet lengths apart. And, lo! You can actually reach the ceiling with a backhand ceiling ball!

That's what I mean by the court diminishing in size as you play more and more. Do you understand what happens when you combine this court shrinkage with the expansion of time that comes with experience? Even if you set up slowly on shots right now, the time will come when setting up becomes almost as routine and unrushed as walking to the shower room.

11. Backpedaling

A common setup error among beginning players is backpedaling in pursuit of shots. The ball comes at them off the front wall and they back up or run in reverse.

Backpedaling causes numerous problems. It is a slow way to move, and you're liable to trip and end up with splinters in your rear cushion. If you don't trip, you are still off balance when you hit the ball—with most of your weight on the rear foot as you continue to backpedal through the swing. In addition, backpedaling contributes to other stroke errors, such as the step-less swing, the push stroke, and lack of body rotation.

The correction consists of turning and moving sideways as you pursue the ball into deep court. As the ball rebounds off the front wall, pull your racquet back into the backswing position and face the sidewall—the right sidewall if you're going to hit a forehand, the left sidewall for a backhand. Then chase the ball with a side stride, as when a basketball player moves laterally when covering an opponent who is dribbling the basketball.

Try the sideways retreat into back court without the ball at first. Start at the short line and pretend a ball has been lobbed over your head. Quickly turn to face the right sidewall, and sidle sideways toward the back wall. Repeat this until the movement becomes natural. Then try the sideways retreat from the short line while facing the left sidewall—as though running down a shot to be hit with your backhand. Note that

Backpedaling. Backpedaling after shots causes numerous problems.

these drills are similar to the back wall shadow retreat exercises described in chapter 9. Got it? Then add the ball. Do the same thing after giving yourself a back wall setup on a lob off the front wall. Turn, retreat sideways, set up, step, and swing.

12. Open Stance

Many hardwood novices hit the ball while facing the front wall. They see the ball coming at them from the front court, and they either just stand there or they backpedal so that as the ball comes into their contact zone, their pelvis and shoulders are pointed at the front wall. This is called an open stance and it is disadvantageous. This incorrect stance limits your swing by not allowing the pelvis and hips to come into play (body rotation). All that swings is the arm, so the net result is a loss of stroke power. In addition, shots hit from an open stance tend to go into the middle of the court or crosscourt. This is a problem when you want to kill the ball since most kill shots should go up and down the line.

Open Stance. Hitting from an open stance when there is ample time to step into a closed stance is disadvantageous because it doesn't allow your lower body to contribute to the swing. This limits stroke power.

One variation of hitting from an incorrect open stance is simply planting the feet during the setup, then not stepping into the ball (into a closed stance).

The worst form of hitting from an open stance is the player who totally faces the front wall when hitting a forehand or backhand. No power at all here.

A problem closely related to hitting from an open stance is stepping into the ball with your rear foot. When you do this, you place your rear foot closer to the near sidewall than your front foot. Hence, stepping into the ball with the rear foot is a form of setting up on a shot in an open stance. It is incorrect.

Correct the open stance or the rear foot lead by facing the right sidewall for forehands or the left sidewall for backhands. Then, in preparation for the swing, step toward the sidewall with your lead foot. This will cause your pelvis and shoulders to face the sidewall when you swing, which takes care of all the symptoms I mentioned earlier. Now your swing will be more natural and use less arm effort. Your body weight will automatically be behind the stroke, and you will tend to hit the ball straight down the line instead of down the middle or cross-court.

The closed stance is such an important concept that I would like you to envision yourself on the court right now to go through a mental rehearsal of the correct technique. Okay, you see the ball coming to your forehand in right deep court. Your initial reaction is to start moving toward the spot at which the ball, after its floor bounce, will descend to knee height. You want to be set and stepping into the ball as it drops into your contact zone. As you move toward this area, you draw your racquet into the backswing position with the wrist cocked. Now you begin to visualize where the ball will be. You turn your body to face the right side-

In this photo sequence, the player is stepping into the ball *(above left)* with her rear foot rather than front foot. Doing this . . .

. . . places the rear foot closer to the near sidewall than the front foot *(above center)*, and . . .

. . . precipitates hitting the ball from an open stance with most of the body weight improperly on the rear foot *(above right)*.

Heather McKay steps into a closed stance to initiate her forehand stroke. Hitting from a closed stance—with the lead foot closer to the near sidewall than the back foot—has several inherent advantages. The swing is more natural and less arm effort is required because the lower body is allowed to contribute to the stroke. The closed stance automatically brings about proper weight transfer, putting body weight behind the stroke. And finally, this closed positioning on the stroke naturally encourages you to hit the ball straight down the line, rather than down the middle of the court or crosscourt. (Charfauros)

wall. Both feet are approximately parallel to each other and about equidistant from that sidewall. Now the ball is descending into your hitting area. You get into the closed stance by moving your lead foot about two feet closer to the right sidewall. Then you swing.

13. Twirly-Twirly

You have probably observed or even performed the twirly-twirly follow-through. This happens when the player sets up for a shot and swings, with her body following her racquet around—and perhaps around again. Typically, however, the twirly-twirly follow-through is a 270- to 360-degree turn. The player ends up facing the left sidewall on forehands, the right sidewall on backhands.

This error is most common among ladies who use what my fellow pro, Jean Sauser, calls a helicopter swing. The helicopter swing involves sticking your arm straight out from your body with a stiff or locked wrist. The ensuing swing is like the rotation of a helicopter-blade. This is what happens: The lack of wrist cock causes no wrist break. This decreases power, so the player must produce stroke power entirely with her upper arm and body, and the helicopter-blade swinging arm pulls the entire body around. The rear leg usually lifts in the air and the ball of the lead foot serves as a pivot. Then, around and around she goes, like a racquet-wielding top.

Twirly-Twirly. This twirly-twirly common error is where the player sets up for a shot, swings with a roundhouse stroke, and her entire body follows her racquet around and around.

The Forehand Twirly-Twirly. The initial swing here is satisfactory, but then . . .

. . . the lead foot acts as a pivot and the body spins around to face the left front corner or, in extreme cases, the left sidewall.

The Backhand Twirly-Twirly. Here comes *(top left)* the ball. This player sets up fine so far, as her initial move *(top center)* was to face the right sidewall. (Note she's a lefty.) And she steps beautifully into a proper closed stance *(top right)* . . .

. . . but then the bad punch line to this stroke *(far left)*—she spins around. Her lead foot acts as a pivot and her rear leg swings improperly around past that front leg *(left)*.

The cure for the twirly-twirly is: Cock your wrist so that you can snap the racquet when you hit the ball. Crook your elbow at ninety degrees on the backswing. Finally, step into a closed stance with your lead foot and don't allow your shoulders to open up so much (face the front wall) on the follow-through.

14. Helicopter Swing

I use Jean Sauser's metaphor for this common error because it is so descriptive. The helicopter begins with a flat, waist-high backswing in which the arm draws back level with the floor and with no wrist cock. The ensuing swing is flat, waist-high, with the arm straight out and with no wrist snap. The follow-through is flat, waist-high, with the arm straight back and with no wrist flex. (The follow-through may or may not continue around for a twirly-twirly.)

The helicopter, like the twirly-twirly, reduces power and puts you off balance on the follow-through. Worse, this stiff-arm swing may put a strain on your elbow. Any joint is more susceptible to strain or other injury when it is locked, as is the elbow joint during the helicopter swing.

Review the correction for the twirly-twirly to remedy the helicopter. It is especially important to crook your elbow at ninety degrees during the backswing. Conjure up the image of a baseball pitcher throwing a ball sidearm. Got it? Now imitate that image with your racquet as

Helicopter Swing. The improper helicopter stroke begins with a flat, waist-high backswing—in which the arm draws the racquet back with little or zilch wrist cock.

you swing at air. Your bent elbow should lead the swing to the potential point of contact, at which time the wrist releases or snaps forward to lead the swing during your follow-through. Listen for the brisk swishing sound of the strings accelerating through the air during the wrist snap. (This auditory clue to faster head speed definitely isn't present during the helicopter swing.)

15. Strokus Interruptus

Perhaps just as common as the twirly-twirly follow-through is the opposite syndrome—the follow-through that is brought to an abrupt stop shortly after ball contact. The stroke just stops as though it runs into a brick wall.

The problem with this strokus interruptus is that you put a heavy strain on your elbow when you bring your swing to a jarring halt. I cringe every time I see this common error committed because I know that the player probably is or will be playing with a sore elbow. It really is like hitting a brick wall in midswing, with the same painful consequences.

The solution is not difficult once you acknowledge that the problem exists. I have found

The start of a forehand helicopter with absolutely no wrist cock.

The start of a backhand helicopter with absolutely no wrist cock.

California pro player Jay Jones demonstrates the cure to the helicopter stroke: (1) Cock your wrist at the top of the backswing, (2) crook your elbow at about ninety degrees at the top of the backswing, and (3) step with your lead foot into a closed stance to initiate the downswing. (Zeitman)

A 360-degree look at the forehand wrist cock.

Strokus Interruptus.

The problem with strokus interruptus is that by bringing your swing to a sudden stop in mid-follow-through, you rob your stroke of its full potential power. A short-stop follow-through usually begins with a short-begin backswing, which is covered in common error 16.

that players who have a stop-short follow-through generally also have a start-short backswing. One seems to beget the other, causing the player to poke at or punch, rather than properly stroke, the ball. The racquetball stroke is not a poke, punch, push, or tap. Do not hit the ball as though putting a shot. Instead, use a longer, more sweeping motion that is interrupted only by the wrist snap at midswing.

Are you still having problems with strokus interruptus on your follow-through? Then try this gimmick: Imagine a string is tied to the end of your racquet. You swing at the ball and just after you contact it an imaginary puppeteer steadily tugs on the string to pull the racquet for a complete follow-through.

Little has been said about the follow-through, since little thought need usually attend it. That is because a proper follow-through is the consequence of a proper swing—not vice versa. This common error—strokus interruptus—illustrates this point particularly well.

A picture-perfect follow-through. The racquetball stroke is not a poke, punch, push, or tap. That is, it is a longer and more sweeping motion that is catalyzed by the wrist snap at midswing.

16. Short Backswing

The obvious common error related to strokus interruptus is the shortened backswing. This mistake is caused either by simply not being in the habit of drawing the racquet back far enough on the backswing, or by not setting up quickly enough on the ball.

Correct the first case of bad habit by giving yourself the mental command before each backswing to pull the racquet back farther and-/or higher. After a couple of days, these mental cues will no longer be necessary since the proper backswing will be established firmly in your subconscious. There is an alternate solution that might have already occurred to you: Entice the imaginary puppeteer to pull your backswing back a little farther. Try 10 percent farther back for a few strokes, then 10 percent more, and so on, until your backswing is deep and high enough.

Correct the second case—setting up too slowly—by, of course, setting up on the shot more quickly. As soon as you see the ball coming at, say, your forehand, get your feet moving so that you arrive at the hitting area before the ball does. Then you'll have time to draw your racquet back into a proper backswing. Refer to the section in this chapter on slow setup (p. 154) for a wealth of information on setting up for shots.

The term "too short a backswing" is somewhat inappropriate since it implies only one dimension—back—with the backswing. Actually, the racquetball backswing involves two directions—height and depth. Height refers to how far above your head the racquet goes. Depth means how far toward the back wall the racquet is drawn. In general, the higher and deeper the backswing, the greater the subsequent stroke power.

You can prove this to yourself. First, test

Short Backswing.

This forehand backswing is plenty deep enough—that is, it is drawn far enough back toward the back wall. But, the backswing is too low. Typically, and in this photo, a lack of wrist cock is seen concurrent with too low a backswing.

Examine these two backswings carefully. The main difference is in the depth of the backswing. Although neither backswing is incorrect, the one in the photo on the right has the racquet drawn back farther. (The heights of the two backswings are fairly equivalent.) The farther (deeper) you draw back your backhand backswing, the more your shoulder and hips turn away from the front wall; that is, the greater the body coil. What effect will this have on stroke power?

depth. You are going to hit shots with a constant height but with a varying depth of backswing. Go through each of the following steps by starting the stroke with a backswing drawn up so that the butt of the handle is ear-high. This is the constant height. Ready? Start with a one-foot-deep backswing and hit four or five shots straight into the front wall. In other words, your backswing starts only one foot behind your point of contact. (Use a normal follow-through.) Note the power of your stroke in terms of ball velocity. Next, start with a two-foot-deep backswing. Hit four or five shots and make a mental note of the power relative to the one-foot backswing in the prior step. Then do the same thing, only with a three-foot backswing. Finally, use a very deep backswing.

Does all this sound familiar? It's the same as stroke add-on steps 5–11, where you discovered that the farther back you take your backswing, the harder you hit the ball. On the final step you took a maximally comfortable backswing, cracked the ball, and smelled burning rubber all the way to the front wall. No odor is more pleasantly fragrant than this racquetball perfume.

Now let's test the effect on power of varying *height* of backswing. You are going to hit four or five shots with the depth of your backswing remaining constant but the height varying. Start each of the swings with your normal depth of backswing—the maximally comfortable depth. Then hit the first series of four or five shots with no height at all on the backswing. That is, your

arm starts back with an absolutely level backswing—about knee high. Note your stroke power. Hit the next four or five shots with a slightly elevated backswing. That is, start the racquet about six inches higher than in the previous step—about six inches above knee height. Again, note your relative stroke power. Then take the racquet up six inches higher, or starting about a foot above knee height. Now hit shots with a very high backswing. What effect did gradually increasing the height of backswing in these steps have on power? On accuracy?

Perhaps you found that increasing the height of backswing had more effect on power than did increasing the depth. Perhaps you experienced just the opposite. Perhaps you lost control with a higher or a deeper backswing. I personally find that taking my racquet farther back increases my power without sacrificing control, whereas taking my racquet farther up on the backswing increases power but decreases accuracy somewhat. I'm not saying that these effects will hold for you. Just how far back or high the backswing can go before you start to lose stroke control is an individual factor that you will discover only through an analytical approach similar to the one outlined above.

The cause and effect of the racquetball backswing are similar to those of hammering a nail or splitting wood with an ax. What happens to power and accuracy when you take different lengths of backswings with these hitting implements?

Kathy Williams zeros in on a ball that hangs off the front wall. Her choked grip and low backswing are giveaways that Williams is a control rather than a power player. The secret is to generate maximum power with maximum control. Experiment: Progressively add 10 percent increments of depth to your normal forehand or backhand backswing, and evaluate the effect on power versus accuracy. Then progressively add 10-percent increments of height to your normal backswing. You'll discover what works best for you only through analytical trial and error. (Bledsoe)

A detailed look at the backhand wrist cock and wrist break. Review the text in add-ons 4 and 6 in chapter 7 if you are having trouble getting wrist into your backhand swings. The cock is up and back. The break is a wrist extension.

17. Underhanded Swing

This error is much more common with the forehand than with the backhand. Whichever stroke you use, swinging underhanded means that you allow the racquet head to tilt down, or fall below the level of your wrist during the downswing. Take a mental snapshot that freezes your forehand stroke right at ball contact. Does the racquet handle angle toward the floor rather

Underhanded Swing.

The underhand swing frequently begins with a very high backswing on the forehand, and . . .

. . . the downswing is improperly underhanded like a pitcher throwing a softball. Contact is made too close to the body with the racquet handle pointed down, and the follow-through is up toward the ceiling rather than fairly parallel with the floor.

than being parallel to it? If so, you are swinging underhanded.

Underhanded strokes bring about undesirable shots. The balls skip into the floor if you happen to make contact too deep—behind the normal contact zone. Or, the balls fly too high into the front wall if you make contact too far forward—in front of your proper contact zone. Thus, underhanded swings lead to a loss of horizontal accuracy. This is bad, because the primary target area in racquetball is a horizontal strip of the front wall that stretches twenty feet from sidewall to sidewall and only a foot up from the floor. This strip is the kill-shot target area, but you'll miss it if you swing underhanded.

Self-diagnosis of the underhanded swing is sometimes difficult because players often feel they are swinging sidearm when, in fact, they are scooping the ball with a softball pitcher's underhanded throwing motion. I recommend that you have a friend take a look at your forehand. If she says you swing like a sidearm baseball pitcher, then you're okay. But if she says you swing like an underhanded softball pitcher, then it's time for a change.

The change to the more level stroke isn't difficult if you follow this two-step process: (1) Put your racquet aside and take the racquetball into your gun hand. Now, pretend you are a sidearm baseball pitcher blazing a fastball at the front wall. Go ahead and throw, remembering that these are fastballs, not change-ups. Repeat until the motion feels comfortable and you get a sense of horizontal or side-to-side accuracy on your throws. (2) Now repeat the same throwing motion, only use your racquet to hit the ball. The throwing and hitting have similar backswings, wrist cocks, downswings, wrist breaks, and follow-throughs—if you are throwing and hitting sidearm. Again, after a few hits you should feel an increase in side-to-side bottom-board control.

You don't like this analogy? Then try imitating a rock skipper. The kinetics of the racquetball forehand are remarkably similar to the sidearm throwing motion used to skip a flat rock across a pond. Picture it, then imitate.

I have not really addressed this common error for the backhand because, as I mentioned, it is much more prevalent on forehands. In addition, the backhand stroke is not quite as much a sidearm stroke as is the forehand. Ideally it is a combination of the baseball pitcher's sidearm throw and the golfer's underhanded swing. Therefore, your racquet handle may angle a bit more toward the floor than with the forehand, though it should not point directly at the floor, because the backhand swing is not entirely underhanded.

The Forehand Wrist Cock and Wrist Break.

The wrist cock is up and back. The wrist break is mostly a flexion, like slapping someone across the face. This photo sequence also brings out another important component of the forehand—a level sweep of the racquet during the wrist snap through the contact zone.

18. Too-High Contact

This common error is almost universal among beginning players. The error appears in two forms: (1) Some players realize they contact the ball above their knees and continue to do so because they think that this is the correct height of contact. This is a height contact error due to ignorance. (2) Other players think they hit the ball at their knees, when in reality they hit it around the waist. Recall the anecdote about my student who kept hitting waist-high shots while insisting she was hitting knee-high shots. I finally told her to hit the ball ankle-high and she started making contact at the knees—which is the height at which I wanted her to hit the ball in the first place. She was the player, you remember, who might logically have called me a miracle worker and smothered my headband with kisses of gratitude. Instead, she had the audacity to suggest that I should have had the insight to tell her to contact the ball at her ankles in the first place, if that's where contact was supposed to be. I term this form of the common error a mistake due to delusion.

This book should long ago have cleared up any ignorance you had on the proper height of contact. Let the ball drop, when you can, to knee height before hitting it. I'm gently suggesting that you may be swinging under the delusion that you are hitting the ball lower than you really are. This book can't cure that misconception. Try a videotape or an objective buddy.

Many players unwittingly reinforce the error

Too-high Contact. Contacting the ball too high means hitting it above the knees when there is ample opportunity to allow it to drop to knee level or lower.

of too-high contact by *bouncing* the ball too high during the drop-and-hit exercises used throughout this book. I emphasize that you must bounce the ball during these drills so that it peaks at about your knees. Then make contact just after the ball peaks—at the knees or lower.

Contacting the ball too high is sometimes due merely to a miscalculation in setting up. For example, rushing forward after the ball or otherwise setting up too close to it may force you to make contact at the waist or above. The next common error deals with this, but for now try to set up deeper in the court on your shots so that the ball has a chance to descend into your contact zone.

19. Overhead Syndrome

This common error comes about when a player rushes forward on a ball to her forehand that would normally be a setup at her knees—if only she gave the ball a chance to fall to knee height. Not only does she contact the ball above her knees, she also hits it with an overhead motion similar to hitting a tennis serve or throwing a baseball overhand. There may be a rudiment of reason behind this overhead tendency among novices. The overhand swing seems natural and powerful to anyone who has tossed a ball in prior sports encounters. Indeed, this stroke is natural and powerful, but in racquetball it is suicidal.

Why suicidal? Two reasons: First, because of the angle of the shot. The flight path of the ball originates at head height or above and aims down at a target area on the front wall near the floor. Geometry, common sense, and experience should tell you that even if you hit the front wall within an inch of the floor, such a shot will rebound off the front wall into the floor and pop high into the air. The result is a setup for the receiver. Second, as you recall from our rock-skipping analogy for the underhanded

The overhead syndrome is often a miscarry-over from tennis, where a similar stroke is used to serve and to volley the ball at the net. There is no place for this stroke on the racquetball court, because there is no net over which the ball must be hit.

Overhead Syndrome. A common error that is cousin to the too-high contact error is the overhead syndrome.

swing, you lose horizontal accuracy when you swing with anything less than a sidearm stroke. The overhead swing is just an underhanded swing turned upside down. The result is the same in either case—your shots skip into the floor or hit too high on the front wall.

Running underneath the ball rather than backing up on it and swinging level at knee height has two other detrimental consequences. First, you tend to hit shots high on the front wall or into the ceiling. Second, you often find yourself off balance and falling backwards (no step into the ball or body rotation) if you run too far underneath the shot.

Correct the overhead syndrome by having patience when setting up on shots. In some cases, it is better to let the ball come to you rather than to attack it with an overzealous charge. Think of yourself as a baseball batter who waits for the ball to come into the strike zone before swinging. If you have trouble lowering your height of contact at first, try doing it gradually. Start with an overhead height of contact and proceed to a chest-high contact, then to a waist-high contact, to a knee-high contact. As you gradually lower your point of contact, you will probably lower the front wall point of contact for your shots. In addition, the lower you contact the ball, the more level the ball's flight to the front wall, which means flatter rollouts.

20. Too-Low Contact

A much less common error, but one worth mentioning, is contacting the ball too low. My preceding explanation might mislead you into believing that if you could contact the ball just a wrist thong's diameter up from the floor, you would get absolutely flat rollouts every time. The defect here is in the stroke, not in the theory. Most players find it difficult to contact the ball that close to the floor without throwing off their strokes. Shoestring-high hitting usually necessitates swinging underhanded, which I have already refuted.

Do your shots consistently skip or go too high into the front wall? Do you find yourself bending uncomfortably at the knees and waist to get way down on the ball? That's too much bend. Straighten up your act and go for knee-high contact.

Too-low Contact. Some players contact the ball down around the soles of their shoes, and they can't understand why their shots either skip into the floor or are lifted too high into the front wall.

21. Getting Down

That leads us to getting down on the ball. The common error here lies in setting up on a shot as though rigor mortis had set in yesterday. There is no flex at the knees, as though you were in double leg casts, and there is no bend at the waist, as if you were wearing a cement corset. How do you expect to get down low enough to hit the ball at knee height if you bend like this?

For many players, a more practical point is *how much* you should bend in getting down on the ball. Well, I've already hinted at the answer to this when I mentioned your physiotype on numerous occasions. Different body builds demand different degrees and points of bending.

There are basically two ways to get down on the ball: bending at your waist, and/or bending at your knees. Lanky women will have to bend more at both places to attain a reasonable knee-high stroke. Shorter players are already down there near the floor and don't have to flex so much at the knees and waist. You see, getting down on the ball is very much an individual thing. No two women on the pro tour get down in exactly the same manner, so I can't give you an exact model to imitate.

My final advice is to be comfortable and natural, and to experiment. Drop and hit some shots while bending a lot. Then drop and hit some more shots from a more upright stance. Which feels more comfortable and natural? Try some shots with a stance in between these two extremes. What about more knee bend, or less? What about more waist bend, or less? The permutations are finite, and there is one correct stance for you. You'll find it if you look hard enough.

Getting Down. Swinging with little bend in the knees or waist is all part of not getting down on the ball.

You have to get down in racquetball if you want the ball to hit low on the front wall. This stretchy lady is about to contact the ball too high due to a lack of bend at the waist.

This player is hitting the ball too high due to a lack of flex both at her waist and her knees.

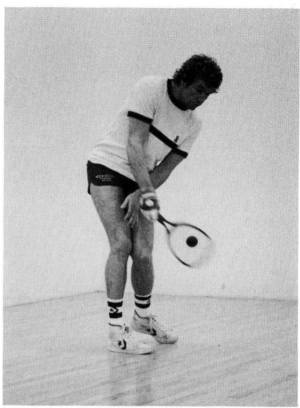

Too-close Contact. Crowding the body on the fore-hand or backhand swing decreases stroke power.

Too-close contact usually forces the swing to be un-derhanded rather than sidearm.

Too-close contact may plague either the forehand or the backhand of a novice player.

When too-close contact is combined with too-high contact, you throw off your swing, plus poke yourself in the ribs with your elbow.

22. Too-Close Contact

This common error plagues a majority of beginning players. Do you crowd yourself on your swings? Admit guilt if you continually elbow yourself on your downswings. Contacting the ball too close to your body jams your stroke, which jacks up swing smoothness. The result is greatly decreased power, not to mention sore ribs.

This problem comes about not because the ball crowds your body, but because *you* crowd the ball while setting up on the shot. Hence, the solution is to set up farther from the ball. Remember that your extended arm and racquet give you at least three feet of reach. Plus, when you step into the closed stance, it puts you at least two more feet closer to the ball. That gives you a total of five feet of extension. Use that extension and do not overrun your contact zone when you set up. Make ball contact comfortably away from your body.

23. Too-Far Contact

A much less common error is contacting the ball too far from the body. I come across only about one such reacher for every five jammers in my clinics.

As in the preceding error, contacting the ball too far from the body usually indicates a problem in setting up. Practice moving closer to the ball before you take your final step into the shot. Be sure that your final step takes you into the closed stance, and then use a proper stroke rather than the stiff-armed helicopter.

24. Too-Deep Contact

Beginning players invariably contact the ball too high and too deep in the stroke. We already talked about a too-high point of contact (see p. 172). Now let's consider contacting the ball too deep in the swing.

This is another ignorance/illusion error, and

The cure to the too-close common error? Just be cognizant of setting up farther from the ball as it comes at you off the front wall. In this photo, the short line with the ball hovering above emphasizes that you should plant your feet well away from the ball.

Too-far Contact.

Reaching out too far for the ball often comes from using a straight-armed helicopter swing . . .

. . . combined with hitting from an open stance, which

. . . may continue with a twirly-twirly follow-through.

Too-deep Contact. An otherwise perfect stroke may be ruined by contacting the ball too deep in the stance.

it is cured with a good dose of awareness. First, let's attack ignorance: Do you know that you should contact the ball no more than a foot behind your lead foot (after you step into the ball)? Now you do. Next, illusion: Now that you realize that you should contact the ball just after it passes your lead foot, do you still insist that you aren't hitting too deep in your stroke? If so, don't take my word that you may be hitting too deep. Have a friend watch you hit, and have her look for the too-deep symptoms I'm about to describe. Take her into the court with you and drop-and-hit a few shots while she scrutinizes your stroke from the side, not from in front or back of you. You say that she agrees with me, that you're hitting too deep? Fine, now you're aware.

If you don't have a friend to diagnose this common error for you, look for these symptoms of the too-deep syndrome.

This error occurs more when a very lively ball is used. In fact, sometimes the lively ball whizzes at you so fast that you're content just to get a racquet on it, even if you must make contact very deep while falling backward. This error, then, may be unavoidable if you play with a superball. But don't go hang yourself by your sports bra just yet. Court exposure seems to provide an immunity to this beginner's scourge, because few intermediates are plagued by the too-deep syndrome and it is extremely rare among the advanced ranks. I'm not suggesting that you must wait for years of experience to layer on your ball-pocked body before you can

When you contact the ball too deep, it is likely that: (1) your weight is on your rear foot throughout the swing, and . . .

. . . the ball comes off the racquet at an angle toward the near sidewall, rather than going straight at the front wall.

cure this malady. You can either practice for hours a day or use a slower ball that allows for more reaction time on every shot.

Contacting the ball too deep in the stroke is magnified when the ball comes off the back wall. The beginner typically sets up too far from the back wall so that when the ball descends to knee height, her body is incorrectly positioned in front of, instead of behind, the sphere. She then has to lean back and reach back with the racquet to scoop the ball in the proper contact area. The shot angles languidly into the sidewall.

The too-deep contact on back wall shots is similarly cured through experience. You'll find, as I alluded to earlier, that the more you play,

Contacting the ball too deep on ceiling shots is analogous to releasing a baseball too early when pitching. In either case, the ball goes higher than intended. In racquetball, this means that your ceiling shots will hit too far from the front wall and subsequently carry too shallow in back court.

the more time expands. This is an Einsteinian way of saying that today the ball may come at you and rebound off the back wall at a certain speed that allows too little time to set up properly on the shot. But a year from now, if a ball comes at you at the same speed, you'll have enough time to wipe your brow on your mini-towel *and* swing.

I don't expect you to surrender to this common error and to wait for experience to cure you with its wonderful expansion of time. That's too long to wait. Besides using a slower ball, you can learn to set up more quickly on shots. Position yourself deeper in the court while waiting for the ball to fall to knee level. Then station yourself behind the ball when you hit it. On back wall shots, move more quickly and closer to the back wall. Plant your foot and move forward with the ball, but not in front of it. Then bash the ball when it dares enter your contact zone.

25. Too-Far-Forward Contact

This common error is usually the companion of another mistake already covered—contacting the ball too far from the body. And, like reaching for the ball, contacting too far forward is relatively rare even among inexperienced players. I estimate that among beginners, ten times as many contact the ball too deep as those who hit too far forward.

Set up closer to the front wall if this common error is yours. The proper point of contact for forehands is a foot behind your lead foot after you have stepped into a closed stance. It is the same for the backhand: hit the ball behind the lead foot. With neither stroke should you make contact in front of the lead foot, or else you'll suffer the consequences I described.

26. Not Watching the Ball

Perhaps the oldest of sports adages is to "keep your eye on the ball." It doesn't matter what the sport or the type of ball; the secret

Too-far-forward Contact.

Contacting the ball too far forward in the stance can abort an otherwise perfect stroke.

Contacting too far forward can occur on your backhand as well as on your forehand.

Contacting the ball too far forward is often the companion of contacting the ball too far away. In this photo, the player is attempting to make ball contact too far ahead of his lead foot as well as too far out from his body. He'd better roll the ball out because it appears he'll end up on the floor with a face full of splinters.

Too-far-forward contact puts you off balance on the follow-through. Besides stubbing your nose on the floor, your shots will tend to go crosscourt.

Not Watching the Ball. It doesn't matter what the sport or the type of ball used, the maxim still holds: "Keep your eye on the ball."

seems to be to glue your eyes to the orb in flight. This holds true in racquetball. Take a look at almost any photo of a pro just as she swings. Her eyes are riveted to the ball with the intensity of a bird eyeballing a fat worm. Handball great Paul Haber once responded to a query on the importance of watching the ball, "I watch the ball all the time—even during time-outs."

Many players catch a glimpse of the ball coming off the front wall, tell themselves they are watching the ball, and later wonder why they get a mis-hit. In my book, watching the ball means picking its flight up as soon as possible after your opponent's shot, and then looking at the sphere right up to the moment it contacts your racquet strings. You may even want to look for the ghost of the ball. This is the place that it dematerialized the instant your racquet hit it. If you can see the ghost, then you are surely watching the ball all the way into the racquet strings.

Finally, it helps many players to watch more than just the ball as it courses off the front wall. Look for the ball's seam or its perky little navel. Again, if you can distinguish these anatomical parts (or even if you are just looking for them), you are surely watching the ball.

A Pictorial Review of How *Not* to Watch the Ball. These players demonstrate the importance of watching the racquetball. Witness their eagle-eye concentration right up to the point of contact. Other less experienced players often only catch a glimpse of the ball zooming off the front wall, they tell themselves they are watching the ball, and then they wonder why they got a mis-hit or inaccurate shot.

27. Paralysis via Analysis

This common error concerns not stroke technique, but the mind's tendency to subdivide the stroke into its constituent parts and then to consider one or more of these individual components with such mental scrutiny that you lose sight of the whole stroke itself. This is racquetball's version of "you can't see the forest for the trees," and it is caused by overanalyzing the details rather than focusing on the big picture.

Paralysis via analysis is discussed further in the next chapter. Until then, realize that you can overload your mental circuits with too much superfluous input. Avoid overthinking.

28. No Practice

The final common error is not practicing or practicing too little. This is a barrier to improvement that many beginning to intermediate players fail to hurdle. It isn't exactly pleasurable to enter the court alone and swat balls to yourself for an eternity. But it isn't a four-walled dungeon, either. We take up the issue of practice in chapter 9.

Paralysis Via Analysis. Some players simply overthink.

No Practice. Not practicing enough, or not at all, is often the mental barrier that prevents an intermediate player from becoming an advanced player. Unrealized potential due to lack of self-motivation is one of the sadder aspects of sports.

SUMMARY

Use this summary list as a checklist for those common errors you need to work on to correct.

1. Improper grip
2. Too much model
3. Backhand run-around
4. Overswinging
5. Shyness syndrome
6. Underswinging
7. Push stroke
8. No body
9. Step-less swing
10. Slow setup
11. Backpedaling
12. Open stance
13. Twirly-twirly
14. Helicopter swing
15. Strokus interruptus
16. Short backswing
17. Underhanded swing
18. Too-high contact
19. Overhead syndrome
20. Too-low contact
21. Getting down
22. Too-close contact
23. Too-far contact
24. Too-deep contact
25. Too-far-forward contact
26. Not watching the ball
27. Paralysis via analysis
28. No practice

Practicing hard yesterday means having no regrets today. Pro Dave Fleetwood is caught in the throes of a muffed shot. Of the two types of solo practice, the professional players engage more in tuning practice since they already know how to swing correctly. (Brundage)

9
Practice

This chapter is divided into three sections: the following introduction, which is basically a word of encouragement on practicing; a section on how to practice, in which you'll learn how to diagnose and correct flaws in your stroke; and practice drills, which give you enough solo and buddy practice routines to keep you busy until a tournament comes around.

INTRODUCTION

Remember that the main objectives of stroke practice are power without overexertion, and thread-the-needle accuracy. You can get past some players by mastering just one or the other of these objectives, but you'll be doomed to eternal court mediocrity unless you learn how to hit them hard while knowing where they're going.

Many players are cognizant of these objectives but get nowhere in the pursuit of them because they practice what they can already do well, rather than working on the things they perform poorly. The general tendency is to walk into the practice court, trot over to the right sidewall, and start drilling drop-and-hit forehands into the front wall. However, the more intelligent path leads to the left sidewall to practice drop-and-hits with your stinking backhand.

But, as I say, few take this less-beaten though more intelligent path. Their egos rather than their racquetball weaknesses guide them. If you are practicing your strong forehand and any passerby in the gallery happens to notice, what does she think? She sees you have a potent forehand and assumes you have an equally potent backhand. But, if the same passerby sees you practicing your miserable backhand, what does she surmise? Not only does she know you have a miserable backhand, but she also assumes you have an equally miserable forehand.

There are two solutions to this problem. First, you can find a court or a time when there are likely to be no nosy passersby. This works on the theory that you aren't really spastic until someone sees you being spastic. The racquetball populace is full of closet spastics, so why not join the crowd by finding a secluded court during an off hour? The second possible solution is just to deny your ego, come out and announce to the world of passersby, "I am spastic! But I don't really care who knows it!" Whichever solution you choose, it's mandatory that you practice your weaknesses before you practice your strengths.

That is not to say that you should never practice the strokes and shots that you already do well. There are two kinds of practice. The first, which I alluded to in the previous paragraphs, is a *learning* practice. Here, you work on what you can't do—your weaknesses. The time that beginning and intermediate players spend drilling should be devoted almost entirely to this learning type of practice. The second type of practice I term *tuning* practice. In this, you drill on what you can already execute fairly well. When you tune a particular stroke or shot, you may make subtle changes in technique, but your primary concern is to maintain that stroke

The Forehand (Rear View). Practice is more fun when you have a real or imaginary target. According to Steve Keeley's box theory, you aim at a large target (the box), while actually you subconsciously zero in on a smaller target area (the bottom board of the front wall). This gimmick can be used in practice or in games. In games, as your shot accuracy gets better, you should shrink the size of the imaginary target boxes sitting in the front corners. Analyze my forehand in this sequence.

or shot. Pro players spend most of their practice time tuning up their game.

There is a bonus, by the way, to the humdrum practice of tuning strokes with hundreds of the same shots with the same strokes from the same positions on the court. (Otherwise I would have gone nuts in the practice court long ago.) A fellow pro best summed up this bonus when he said, "When you go into the court and work for hours on what you already know, sooner or later you'll discover what you don't know."

Becoming proficient at racquetball has three requirements: (1) You must know what the correct techniques are; (2) you must practice those techniques alone in the court; and (3) you must use those practiced techniques in a game situation. Let's look at where you stand right now regarding these three requirements: (1) You know the correct techniques—from reading this book; (2) you have plenty of practice drills to work on—in the third section of this chapter; and (3) everyone likes to play the game—so, you need no motivation here.

Actually, many players unwittingly neglect requirement number three—practicing the correct techniques in a game situation. If you have any hope of improving, you should work on specifics when you play your buddies in informal games. That is, if you spent an hour alone yesterday practicing your back wall forehand

When you win, nothing hurts and nothing else exists. Pro Francine Davis erupts in victory with a jubilant upswing. Davis spent the first couple of years in the four-wall world as a relatively unknown player. But she practiced and she persevered, and she became a relatively well-known player. (Oram)

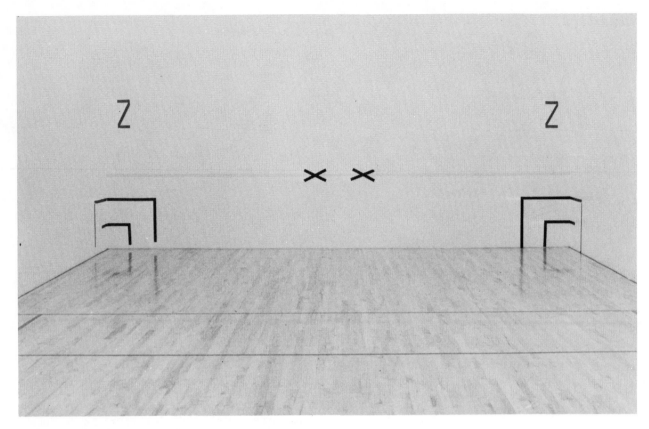

The court with the built-in box theory. Marked courts are becoming fairly commonplace in private clubs across the country. In this practice court the Zs are the target areas for Z-serves, the sideways Xs are drive serve targets, the horizontal line is the upper limit for passes, and the concentric boxes in either corner provide bull's-eyes for kill shots.

kill shot into the right front corner, doesn't it make sense that today you should specifically hit that same kill shot whenever you get a forehand setup off the back wall? Sure it does.

If you didn't practice alone yesterday, you can still practice specific shots or techniques in today's game. This is especially recommended if you play a certain individual on a day-to-day basis, or if your opponent happens to be far less skillful than you. For example, you might want to determine secretly to yourself before the game that you are going to work specifically on your backhand pass shot up and down the left line. Then you go into the game and do just that, though it may mean squandering juicy backhand setups that you would normally kill.

This brings up picking an opponent for your practice games. The big search around any club involves looking for someone better to play.

And this *should* be every serious player's goal—finding a playing partner who is better, but not too much better, than you are. You want to improve, but you don't want to get depressed.

Thus, "playing up" is everyone's major concern. A "C" player wants to play "B" players, a "B" player wants to play "A" players, and so on. This is as it should be, because a better player makes you work harder to score points and the pace of her shots is quicker so that you develop faster reflexes. Also, her control is superior so that you have to really hustle, and you are forced to hit better shots yourself because she returns most of your usual winners. Moreover, there is the undeniable occurrence of talent osmosis out there on the court. You indeed play better against better opponents. You consciously and unconsciously observe which techniques and tactics make them superior players, and

Who knows what worlds exist behind the front wall? No, those aren't square windows to another universe. They're glass partitions for television cameras. Like the real or imaginary boxes in the box theory, they serve as kill shot bull's-eyes. Most forehand kills should go into the forehand corner. And, as I'm about to demonstrate in this photo, most backhand kills should go into the backhand corner. (Ektelon and Phillips Org.)

For a smaller target area, . . .

. . . try zeroing your kill shots in on . . .

. . . a couple of empty cans of balls stacked in the front corner.

Becoming proficient at racquetball has three requisites: knowing the correct techniques, practicing those techniques alone, and practicing those techniques in a game situation. While pursuing these three requisites, it is advantageous to solicit feedback on your techniques. Feedback can be something as sophisticated as a videotape complete with competent instructor, or something as mundane as your day-to-day practice buddy. (Scott)

soon these techniques and tactics become your own.

Unfortunately, reverse talent osmosis also occurs when you "play down" or go against an inferior rival. Who wants to play some spastic who can at best score only five points against Humpty Dumpty? *You* should! It isn't all that bad. For one thing, it's good to take a break now and then from playing better players. Otherwise, depression sets in after, say, two hundred straight losses, and you may drown yourself in the jacuzzi. For another thing, it is easier to work on specific shots against an inferior player. You can try shots and strategies that you normally wouldn't. There is a final advantage to playing down. After a while you relax, you gain confidence, and you decide not to drown yourself in the jacuzzi.

HOW TO PRACTICE

Some may criticize my add-on method of teaching and this section on how to practice. These people will point out that it is faulty to presume that any whole system, such as a stroke, can be understood completely through an orderly assault on its constituent elements, such as the stroke add-ons. I don't deny this. I have insinuated throughout that stroke work is a science *and* an art, and any art requires more than a part-by-part analysis to be understood and learned.

Unfortunately, I know no better way to teach and to learn how to practice the strokes. I can only provide you with the sequence of constituent elements that comprise the strokes, then hope you can put them together to come up with art. Therefore, I am not apologizing for my teaching approach. I merely want you to be aware that learning and practicing according to this technique may result in a couple of problem areas. They are paralysis via analysis (see page **182**) and a **mechanical swing.**

Paralysis via analysis is not always self-induced; there may be outer influences. Let me give you an example of *forced* paralysis via analysis. One of the oldest psychological ploys in the unwritten book of gamesmanship involves commenting in an offhanded manner about some particular aspect of an opponent's stroke. The male pros of yesteryear used this psychological gambit all the time back in the days when gamesmanship held an upper hand to sportsmanship. Typically, one player would offer aloud, "Oh, *that's* very interesting." The opponent would then take the bait: "*What's* very interesting?" Then, "Oh, nothing really. I was just noticing how you gripped the racquet with your thumb against your middle finger." That's when the paralysis via analysis set in. The deceived player often began thinking to himself, "What's so interesting about my thumb being on my middle finger? That's where it's *supposed*

to be . . . isn't it? So what if it isn't? I don't care, and I won't let it affect my game!" But by now the guy has fretted over this grave inconsequentiality to the point that it has indeed affected his game.

A mechanical swing is another thing you have to beware of when you learn and practice the strokes via their component add-ons. Oh, there is a certain beauty in mechanical perfection, but it is not artistry. Less than 10 percent of the pro players could be classified as mechanical players whose success comes from pure execution of strokes that have been well oiled and tuned through thousands of practice shots. These players must be admired for their textbook-perfect strokes, but they definitely are not as much fun to watch as are the free-swinging pros who operate on instinct. To witness these latter players in action is to observe movement as a whole, rather than movement broken down into its component parts. If there are component parts in the swings of these instinctual players, they are minute and subtle. They are a hundred thousand add-ons that are small perfect movements, and because they are perfect they go unnoticed.

However, I'm afraid these artsy strokers are a rare breed. You, I'll bet, are more mechanical by nature—which is just fine. Don't worry about it, because there is nothing to be done about it except to avoid paralysis via analysis and an

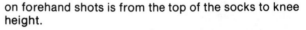

Height of Contact (Forehand): too low *(left)*, too high *(center)*, *(right)* just right! The proper height of contact on forehand shots is from the top of the socks to knee height.

Contact Distance from Body (Forehand): too close . . .

. . . too far away . . .

. . . just right! Hit forehand shots comfortably away from your body. The exact distance varies with the player's height and stroke.

Depth of Contact (Forehand): too deep . . .

. . . too far forward . . .

. . . just right! The proper depth of contact for forehand shots is a few inches behind the heel of the lead foot, after you have stepped into the stroke.

overly mechanical swing. My add-on teaching method is tailor-made for you. And so is the following *component guideline*, which provides those facets of the stroke which you should consider for experimentation. The stroke can be broken down into myriad constituents, but only a few of these are worth testing in quest of stroke improvement.

1. Contact Zone

You should definitely experiment with contacting the ball in various areas. There are three dimensions in pinpointing the center of the contact zone: height of ball contact, depth of ball contact, and distance from the body that you contact the ball. Experiment with these

individually and in conjunction with one another to discover where your ideal contact zone lies.

2. Step into the Ball

There are many different ways to step into a closed stance when striding into the swing. You can step a little more forward, deeper, farther away, or closer; or you can try any combination of these. An inch of difference in your step can cause a major change in your stroke.

3. Body Rotation

Experiment with different amounts of body rotation on the backswing. Does it help to wind

Height of Contact (Backhand): too low . . .

. . . too high . . .

. . . just right! Hit your backhand kills and passes from top-of-sock to knee height.

Contact Distance from Body (Backhand): too close . . .

. . . too far away . . .

. . . just right! As with forehands, hit your backhand shots comfortably away from your body.

Depth of Contact (Backhand): too deep . . .

. . . too far forward . . .

. . . just right! Theoretically, since you hit backhands with your lead arm which is closer to the front wall, your backhand point of contact should be slightly forward relative to your forehand point of contact. Nonetheless, this contact zone should still be behind (toward the back wall) your lead foot after you step into the stroke.

up in the exaggerated manner of a human corkscrew? Or, are your shots better when you coil only slightly, like a timid rattlesnake?

4. Backswing

You can hammer a nail harder when you take a higher backswing. See if the same is true with a racquet and ball. Then decide if the increased power is worth the decrease in control. How about a deeper backswing? A flatter backswing? A loop backswing?

5. Swing Force

It is astonishing how many times I have improved students' strokes by telling them one simple thing: swing harder. It is easier to drum quickly than slowly. A bicycle is more stable when it is pedaled quickly rather than slowly. Similarly, your racquetball swing may become smoother if you put just a little more effort into it. Don't go for an all-out flail or you'll strain your arm. Add 10 percent more swing power to your present stroke and see what it does. Then add 10 percent more, and so on.

On the other hand, I have also diagnosed some players' stroke problems as overswinging. If you suspect you are swinging too hard, try letting up just 10 percent on your stroke and see what happens. Then let up 10 percent more, and so on.

6. Wrist Cock

The basic wrist cock is up and back. That doesn't mean there isn't room for innovation. There are varying degrees the wrist can be cocked in both directions. And, there are different combinations of these various degrees of direction.

7. Bending

There are two ways to get down on the swing so that you can take a coordinated swat at a ball knee-high or below: you can bend at the knees, or at the waist. Different physiotypes and strokes demand different areas and amounts of bending. Try more knee bend, then less. Try more waist bend, then less. Then combine different amounts of knee bend with different amounts of waist bend.

Somehow, it's never the same during the match as it is when you're alone on the practice court. Don Thomas attempts to swing under the legs of Hogan. This Hogan-Thomas match has a lesson: Don't be afraid to play someone—in practice or in competition—who is supposed to be better than you. Every serious player's goal around the court club should be to find a practice partner who is better, but not too much better. (You want to improve, but you don't want to get depressed.) And remember that the bigger they are, the harder they fall. Thomas defeated Hogan in this match, the first player to knock down the kingpin in two years on the pro circuit. (Brundage)

8. Footwork

There is more footwork, less footwork, and everything in between. Try using exaggerated footwork when setting up on a shot, like an Indian doing a rain dance. Then try setting up with less footwork, like a wooden Indian cruising a tobacco shop.

9. Grip

I place this point last on the list because I hesitate to include it at all. Get your grip down *before* you practice your strokes. If your grip is correct, there is usually no need to experiment with it. I'd rather have you try out a different backswing, wrist cock, or whatever.

Still, there is a real potential for a slight change in grip, causing a major change in the way the ball comes off your racquet strings. You may try moderate variations of the height of your grasp, or the amount of handle rotation within your hand (altering the placement of the thumb-index finger V). But heed these two warnings: Do not deviate far from the model forehand and backhand grips, and don't forget how you were holding the racquet before you started experimenting with the grip.

Racquetball is a game of inches, and the racquetball stroke consists of a series of delicately interrelated movements. If you consciously or unconsciously make a minor adjustment in your swing, you can throw your shots off (or on) by those inches. Don't scoff the details. Let me give you a personal case in point. A couple of years ago, I had the forehand blues. This was the worst kind of stroke problem in that my shots were alternately good and bad, but they all *felt* bad. In other words, I had no concrete symptoms, no diagnosis, and no cure to take into the practice court and drill into my nervous system. Then, one day after weeks of fruitless practice, I came across an old magazine picture of me hitting a forehand— back when my forehand was "on." I took particular note of how strange my hitting elbow looked as it swept past my body during the downswing. It almost jammed me in the ribs as I swung. Just for kicks, I went onto the court and tried it. It worked! Suddenly I remembered what I have told at least a dozen students in the past: "Your elbow leads the stroke and stays fairly close to your body during the downswing."

My point here is not to advise you to keep your elbow in on the forehand. Rather, my point is that the slightest adjustment in any of the stroke aspects listed in the preceding component guideline can prove highly rewarding. I urge you to experiment with the details.

Beginning and intermediate players often simultaneously discover two or more weak links in their chain of movements that compose the stroke. There is a proper two-step method to handle stroke correction when more than one change is to be made: (1) Define the changes to be made. Let's say that you want to learn to contact the ball deeper in your stroke, and to take a higher backswing. (2) Determine in which order to make the adjustments. Do not attempt to make both corrections at the same time. I repeat, work on one problem until it is corrected, then go on to the next. Okay, pick out the easiest correction to work on initially, then the next easiest, and so on to the most difficult. In our example above, it is much easier and quicker to change the backswing than it is to move the point of contact. Therefore, you would first work on raising your backswing. When you no longer had to think about doing this, then you would work on moving the point of contact deeper in your stroke.

Now let's get on with the practice drills themselves. The list here is not complete—it never is.

Make up new routines when you get bored with these.

The number of shots to hit for each drill is up to you and should be determined by your budget for court time, the amount of court time available, your patience for solo drilling, your purpose in practicing, and the extent of your desire to improve. I have used an X to indicate the number of shots to hit in each drill. For example, in the first kill shot drill, it says, "Repeat X times." Fill in your own number of shots for the X.

It is important in all the drop-and-hit types of practice drills to . . .

. . . catch the ball after each swing. Then drop and hit again.

BACK-WALL DRILLS

1. Shadow Play

You don't need a partner or a ball to practice back-wall shots, so this routine omits these factors, enabling you to concentrate solely on your footwork—the nemesis of most novice back-wall hitters. You are going to work on the retreat toward the back wall, as well as on the (imaginary) swing.

Stand on the short line in the middle of the court facing the front wall. Pretend someone has just lobbed a ball over your head into the rear forehand corner. That's your call to action. In a continuous motion, turn sideways to face the right sidewall, take your racquet back into the forehand backswing position, and shuffle toward deep court after the imaginary ball. Plant your right foot about three feet from the back wall, reverse your direction of travel, and swing. Hit an imaginary down-the-line *forehand* kill. Repeat X times.

Now perform the same exercise with your *backhand*. Start on the short line in the center of the court and pretend an imaginary lob goes over your head into the rear backhand corner. Do a similar retreat to the back wall, swing, and hit an imaginary down-the-line forehand kill into the left front corner. Repeat X times.

2. Toss and Hit, Back Wall First

Stand in the right rear corner of the court approximately five feet from the back wall and five feet from the right sidewall. Now gently toss the ball into the back wall about five feet above the floor. As the ball rebounds off the back wall, move forward with it. Continue moving with the ball as it bounces off the floor and then descends into your proper contact zone. Hit the shot up and down the *forehand* line. As your accuracy increases, kill the ball up and down the line. Repeat X times.

Now move to a similar position in the left rear of the court—about five feet from the back wall and five feet from the left sidewall. Toss and hit the ball with your *backhand* up and down the left line.

The toss-and-hit (back wall first on the toss) drill for improving back wall play.

3. Toss and Hit, Floor First

Start at the same position for the forehands in the previous exercise. This time toss the ball into the floor first at a spot about two feet from the back wall. It will bounce off the floor into the back wall, then come off for a setup. Use your *forehand* to shoot the ball up and down the forehand alley. As before, hit the front wall first with your shot. As you gain control and confidence, start killing the shots low into the right front corner. Repeat X times.

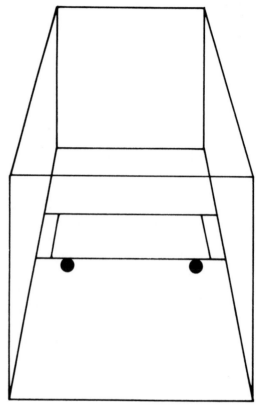

The starting stance for backwall drills—shadow play and setups off the front wall. It is very important that you initiate movement on or near the short line. This allows you to work on footwork, which is the major nemesis of most novice back wall hitters.

The toss and hit (floor first on the toss) drill for back wall play.

Now move to the opposite side of the court and perform the same exercise with your *backhand.* Repeat X times.

4. Setup and Hit

Start on the short line about five feet from the right sidewall. Face the front wall. Lob the ball into the front wall about two-thirds of the way above the floor so that the rebound carries straight back, hits the floor near three-quarters court, then bounces into the back wall and off for a *forehand* setup. This setup shot is the most difficult part of this routine for many. Practice the setup solely a few times without returning the back wall setup—just catch it. When the setting up becomes routine for you, start practicing your forehand back wall shots. That is, follow your lob off the front wall to back court. Plant as the ball rebounds off the back wall, let the ball descend into your contact zone, and swing. Aim your shot up and down the forehand line. Repeat X times.

Now start on the short line about five feet from the left sidewall. Give yourself a lob setup that comes off the back wall in the left rear corner. Hit the ball with your *backhand* up and down the line. Repeat X times.

KILL SHOT EXERCISES

1. Drop and Hit

Start at position A on the court—an arm-and-racquet's length from the right sidewall, and near the short line. Drop and hit the ball with your *forehand* at the peak of its knee-high (or lower) bounce. Kill the ball in the right front corner, hitting the front wall first within three feet of the right sidewall. Aim for less than a foot high on the front wall, lowering this height as you gain more confidence and accuracy. Catch the rebound. Repeat X times.

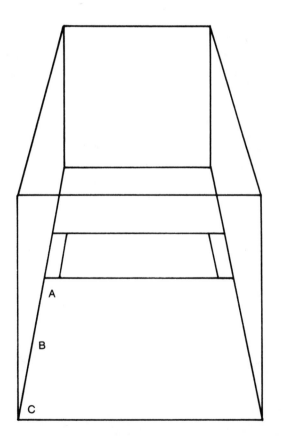

The three starting positions for the forehand drop-and-hit and set-up-and-hit drills. Hit shots until you feel comfortable and confident, then move to a deeper starting position.

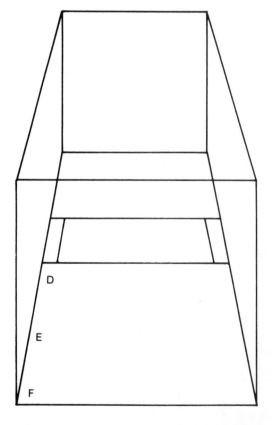

The three starting stations for the backhand drop-and-hit and the set-up-and-hit drills. As with the forehand drills, catch the ball after each shot, then drop and hit or set up and hit again.

Now go to position B on the court, which is still an arm-and-racquet's length from the right sidewall, but ten feet deeper into the court—midway between the short line and the back wall. Perform the same drop-and-hit exercise X times from this position. Remember to catch the ball after each hit, rather than hitting the rebound back into the front wall.

Now retreat to position C on the court. This is still an arm-and-racquet's length from the right sidewall, but about five feet from the back wall. Drop and hit X shots from here to complete the three-position forehand routine.

You may now repeat the above routine for additional forehand drilling, or you can go on and practice your *backhand* kills. Drop and hit with your backhand X shots each from positions D, E, and F. Position D is an arm-and-racquet's length from the left sidewall, and near the short line. Position E is ten feet deeper into the court, about midway between the short line and the back wall. Position F is deeper into the court—about five feet from the back wall.

The forehand drop-and-hit is the most basic of all stroke drills. Study this sequence and analyze my stroke. If this were your stroke, what areas would you improve? How would you go about it? The number of shots to hit on each exercise is up to you. It depends on your available court time, your practice purpose, your patience, and your desire to excel.

2. Set Up and Hit

The three positions—A, B, and C—for this exercise are the same as for the previous drill. Give yourself a soft setup off the front wall and wait for the ball to come at you. As it does, move into position so that you will be able to stroke it with your *forehand* below your knees. Hit the front wall first within three feet of the right sidewall and a foot or less above the floor. Catch the rebound. Repeat X times each from position A, position B, and position C.

You may now repeat the above three-position routine for additional forehand drilling, or you can practice your *backhand* kills. Set up and hit X backhand shots each from positions D, E, and F. These starting stations are on the left side of the court, as in the previous exercise.

3. Front Wall–Sidewall Angle Drill

Start in position G, which is on the short line midway between the sidewalls. Bounce the ball and hit yourself an easy setup that strikes the front wall first about six to eight feet up and a couple of feet from the right sidewall. The ball will carom into the right sidewall and back at you. Move so that you are set to hit the ball when it descends to below your knees. Aim your *forehand* kill into the front wall first—less than a foot high and within a couple of feet of the right sidewall. Catch the return and repeat X times.

Now, from the same position and off the

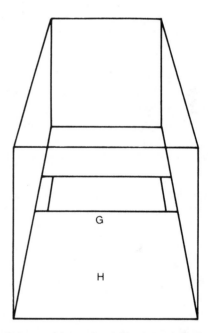

The starting positions for kill shot drill 3. These stations on the court get you used to using the sidewalls on kill shots.

same setup, kill forehands into the sidewall first—less than a foot high and within a couple of feet of the front wall. Catch the returns. Repeat X times.

Repeat this drill if you desire more forehand work. Otherwise, start the *backhand* front wall–sidewall angle drill. The position G starting station is the same as before. Now, however, direct your kills into the front wall a couple of

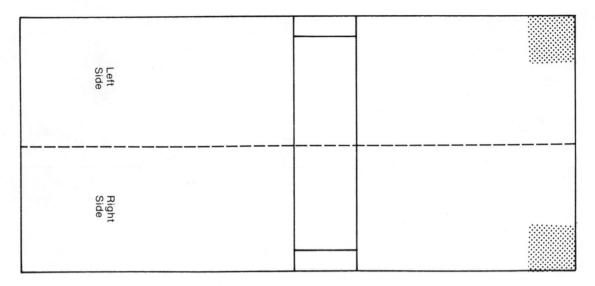

All the kill shot practice drills have a strategic basis. Assume that the court is divided into equal left and right halves. Kill shot strategy demands that you aim your roll-offs into the near corner. This means that shots killed from the right half of the court generally go into the right front corner, and balls from the left side are usually directed into the left front corner.

feet from the left, or backhand, sidewall. Kill X shots into the front wall first as before, only this time use your backhand.

Now, from the same two positions and off the same setups, kill your backhands into the sidewall rather than the front wall first. Repeat X times.

This time, do the same front wall–sidewall angle drill, only from a deeper position in the court. This position H is about midway between the sidewalls and midway between the short line and the back wall. Set up and hit X shots with your forehand, killing into the front wall first. Next, kill X forehands into the right sidewall first.

Now do the same with your backhand into the left front corner. Set up and kill X shots into the front wall first, then X into the left sidewall first.

PASS SHOT EXERCISES

1. Down-the-Line Drop and Hit

Perform this exercise with just your backhand on the left side of the court. (The forehand down-the-liner is usually unwise, so it makes no sense to practice it.) This is the same as exercise one for backhand kill shots, except now you are going to drop and pass the ball up and down the backhand alley. Use the same three positions as in the backhand kill shot exercise—D, E, and F. Drop and hit X down-the-line passes from each of these, catching the rebounds. Aim for a target area on the front wall two to four feet above the floor and within three feet of the left sidewall.

2. Down-the-Line Set Up and Hit

Again, do this exercise with just your backhand on the left side of the court. This is the same as exercise two for backhand kill shots, except now you are going to hit down-the-line passes off those setups from the front wall. Use

The backhand drop-and-hit. Assuming your backhand is your weaker stroke, you'll no doubt spend many hours practicing this and the backhand set-up-and-hit drill. It is imperative that you work on specifics when you practice while you are in the learning phase of your court career. Working on specifics may mean correcting your backhand backswing, instead of correcting your overall backhand stroke. It may mean experimenting with different heights or depths of contact on the drive serve, rather than working on the drive serve as a whole. Furthermore, it is important that you work on your weaknesses, giving less practice time to your strengths. This means that if you have a strong forehand, work on your backhand. If you have a good Z-serve, work on your drive serve.

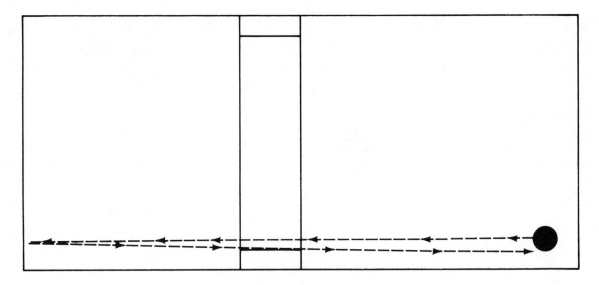

Backhand pass shots should generally be hit down the left line. The pass practice drills encourage this.

the same three positions as in the backhand kill shot drill—D, E, and F. Set up and hit X passes along the left sidewall from each of these stations, catching the rebound. The front wall bulls-eye is again two to four feet above the floor and within three feet of the left sidewall.

3. Perpetual Down-the-Line Drill

This is an advanced exercise, more difficult than the first two pass drills. Perform it with only your backhand on the left side of the court. Start at position F—about five feet from the back wall and five feet from the left sidewall. The object is to carry on a down-the-line pass rally with yourself. Drop and hit the first pass, then continue hitting down-the-line passes off the subsequent setups. The total pass count before an error ends a rally is a good measuring stick of progress. Repeat for X solo rallies.

4. Down-the-Line Buddy Drill

This is another advanced routine to be done with only the backhand on the left side of the court. This is the same as the preceding perpetual down-the-line solo drive drill, only now you use a partner rather than hitting alone. One of you initiates the rally by dropping and hitting a pass up and down the left alley. The other

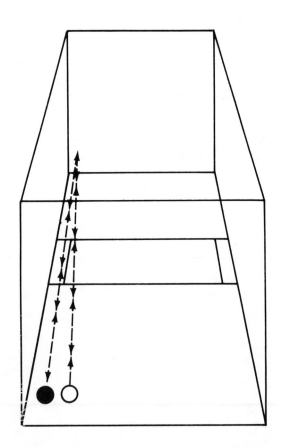

The perpetual down-the-line pass drill with two players not only increases backhand control, but you also get a workout.

player returns with another alley drive, and the down-the-line rally continues until one player errs. Then, the ball is caught and you start again. Repeat for X rallies.

5. Crosscourt Set Up and Hit

The starting station for the forehand drill is anywhere in the right rear quadrant of the court. If you need a more specific location, begin at position C—about five feet from the right sidewall and five feet from the back wall. Give yourself an easy setup off the front wall and hit a forehand crosscourt pass. The drive should hit the front wall two to four feet high and about midway between the sidewalls. If angled correctly, your pass will carry into the left rear corner near the sidewall–back wall vertical crack juncture. Lower the front wall bulls-eye if your shots come off the back wall. Retrieve the ball, and repeat X times. It is more efficient to use two, three, or a bag of balls for this drill.

6. Crosscourt Buddy Drill

You and your practice partner assume starting stances at around three-quarters court, one player five feet from the right sidewall and the other five feet from the left sidewall. One player drops and hits a crosscourt pass to the other player, and the latter returns it with a crosscourt pass. You and your buddy thus act as mutual ball-return machines, and a crosscourt pass rally perpetuates. Strive for control on this exercise rather than trying to smash the ball past each other. Catch the ball after a mis-hit. Repeat this buddy routine for X rallies. This exercise is especially valuable for a righty and lefty who each want to work on the backhand crosscourt pass.

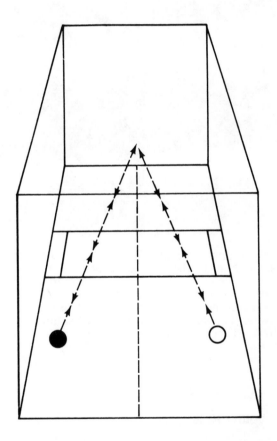

The crosscourt buddy pass drill is an exercise in racquet control. Keep your passes low—no higher than three feet—on the front wall so the ensuing rebound will not carry off the back wall. It may help on all passes, whether hit in practice or during a game, to imagine a horizontal line drawn across the front wall (from sidewall to sidewall) three feet up from the floor. Don't let your passes hit above this imaginary line.

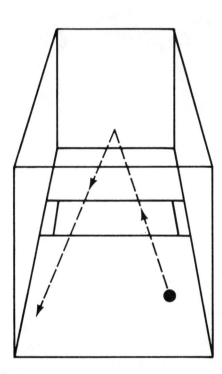

The crosscourt pass drill is generally done with the forehand from the right side of the court. Aiming forehand passes crosscourt in practice makes you remember to do the same in the hurry-scurry of a game.

Some say that multinational champion Charley Brum-field lives in another world. He has insight into the game and is far-seeing, it is said, while the rest of the hardwood community wears thick spectacles. Others venture further in stating that Brumfield is somewhere between a genius and a crazy man. What other type of person (it is said) could practically live in a court for a decade, making it his castle? (Brundage)

VOLLEY EXERCISES

1. Volley Kills

The court stations for the *forehand* volleys are positions A and B on the right side of the court. Start at position A on the short line near the right sidewall and give yourself a setup off the front wall that carries to you in the air—without a floor bounce. Contact the ball waist-high and kill straight into the right front corner.

Retrieve the ball and repeat X times.

Back up about ten feet to position B. Set up and volley X kill shots. Note that there is usu-ally no position C for this exercise. You should not volley the ball so far from the front wall; let it go for a back-wall setup.

Now move over to the left side of the court to practice volley kills with your *backhand*. Hit X shots from position D on the short line. Then, X shots from position E deeper in the court.

Appendices

Appendix A
Answers to Quiz

Below are the answers to the quiz given in Chapter One. See page 20 to review the questions.

1. a
2. False. The serve must hit the front wall first.
3. False. It must hit between the short line and the back wall.
4. d
5. False. Only the server scores.
6. False. The serve return does not have to hit the front wall first.
7. A point for the server, or a side-out for the receiver.
8. Yes.
9. False. The server must step outside the service box for a foot fault to be called.
10. False. The receiver wins only the right to serve.
11. Hitting the ball before it bounces on the floor.
12. Ten seconds.
13. False. This is a three-wall serve, which is a side-out.
14. Eleven points.
15. d
16. A side-out. The server loses her serve.
17. Two faults.
18. True.
19. Short serve, long serve, foot fault, ten-second rule.
20. Four.
21. e
22. Twenty by twenty by forty feet.
23. b
24. No. The first player to reach 21 points wins.
25. a

SELF-EVALUATION (BASED ON NUMBER OF CORRECT ANSWERS)

24–25—Pro player
21–23—Open player
18–20—A player
15–17—B player
12–14—C player
 9–11—Novice player
Less—Study the rules

Appendix B
Racquetball Organizations

American Professional Racquetball
Organization (APRO)
730 Pine
Deerfield, IL 60015

Racquetball's equivalent of the U.S. Professional Tennis Association (USPTA). It organizes, tests, and certifies racquetball instructors.

Canadian Racquetball Association (CRA)
333 River Rd.
Vanier City, Ontario,
Canada KIL 8B9

Canada's national sport-governing body for racquetball unites and is the mouthpiece for players in that country. Publishes a magazine for members.

International Racquetball
Association (IRA)
5545 Murray Rd.
Memphis, TN 38117

The first national racquetball organization that caters mainly to amateur players. Includes state organizations, sponsors tournaments, and publishes a member magazine.

National Paddleball Association (NPA)
P.O. Box 712
Flint, MI 48501

The unifying force of paddleball. Runs tournaments and publishes a newsletter.

National Racquetball Clinics, Inc.
10251 Scripts Ranch Rd.
San Diego, CA 92123

The largest clinic group composed of the game's top names. Offers instructional clinics and exhibitions.

National Racquetball Club (NRC)
4101 Dempster St.
Skokie, IL 60076

The association most responsible for the rise of professional racquetball. Implements pro tours and publishes a monthly magazine.

United States Racquetball Association (USRA)
4101 Dempster St.
Skokie, IL 60076

The amateur arm of the NRC. Has a network of state affiliations that oversees racquetball on the amateur level.

Women's Professional Racquetball Association
(WPRA)
3727 Centennial Circle
Las Vegas, NV 89121

Organization of many of the women professional players that seeks to upgrade the existing pro tour, support present sponsors, and solicit new sponsors.

Appendix C
Official Rules

PART 1. THE GAME

Rule 1.1—Types of Games. Racquetball may be played by two or four players. When played by two it is called "singles"; and when played by four, "doubles."

Rule 1.2—Description. Racquetball is a competitive game in which a racquet is used to serve and return a ball.

Rule 1.3—Objective. The objective is to win each rally by serving or returning the ball so the opponent is unable to keep the ball in play. A rally is won when a side is unable to return the ball before it touches the floor twice.

Rule 1.4—Points and Outs. Points are scored only by the serving side when it serves an ace or wins a rally. When the serving side loses a rally, it loses the serve. Losing the serve is called a "side-out" or "hand-out."

Rule 1.5—Game. A game is won by the side first scoring 21 points.

Rule 1.6—Match. A match is won by the side first winning two games.

Rule 1.7—Tie-breaker. In the event each side wins a game, the third game will be won by the side first scoring 11 points. This 11-point third game is called "tie-breaker."

PART II. COURT AND EQUIPMENT

Rule 2.1—Court. The specifications for a standard four-wall racquetball court are:

(a) **Dimensions.** The dimensions shall be 20 feet wide, 20 feet high and 40 feet long with each back wall at least 12 feet high.

(b) **Lines and Zones.** Racquetball courts shall be divided and marked on the floors with 1½ inch wide red or white lines as follows:

(1) Short Line. The short line divides the court in half, parallel to the front and back walls. The back edge of the short line shall be equal distance between the front and back walls, 20 feet from both.

(2) Service Line. The service line is parallel with the short line with the front edge of the service line 5 feet in front of the back edge of the short line.

(3) Service Zone. The service zone is the space between the outer edges of the short line.

(4) The service box lines are located at each end of the service zone and designated by lines 18 inches from and parallel with each side wall.

(5) Service Boxes. The service boxes are the spaces between the side walls and the service box lines.

(6) Receiving Lines. Five feet back of the short line, vertical lines shall be marked on each side wall extending 3 inches from the floor. The back edges of the receiving lines shall be 5 feet

from the back edge of the short line.

Rule 2.2—Ball Specifications. The specifications for the standard racquetball are:

(a) **Size:** The ball shall be 2¼ inches in diameter.

(b) **Weight:** The ball shall weigh approximately 1.4 ounces.

(c) **Bounce:** The ball shall bounce 68–72 inches from a 100-inch drop at a temperature of 76 degrees F.

(d) **Official Ball:** The official ball of the U.S.R.A. is the black Seamco 558; the official ball of the N.R.C. is the green Seamco 559; or any other racquetball deemed official by the U.S.R.A. or N.R.C. from time to time.

Rule 2.3—Ball Selection. A ball shall be selected by the game referee for use in each match in all tournaments. During a game the referee may, at his discretion or at the request of both players or teams, select another ball. Balls that are not round or which bounce erratically shall not be used.

(a) In tournament play, the referees all choose at least two balls for use, so that in the event of breakage, the second ball can be put into play immediately.

Rule 2.4—Racquet. The official racquet will have a maximum head length of 11 inches and a width of 9 inches. These measurements are computed from the outer edge of the racquet head rims. The handle may not exceed 7 inches in length. Total length and width of the racquet may not exceed a total of 27 inches.

(a) The racquet must include a thong which must be securely wrapped on the player's wrist.

(b) The racquet frame may be made of any material, as long as it conforms to the above specifications.

(c) The strings of the racquet may be gut, monofilament, nylon or metal.

Rule 2.5—Uniform. All parts of the uniform, consisting of shirt, shorts and socks, shall be clean, white or of bright colors. Warm-up pants and shirts, if worn in actual match play, shall also be white or of bright colors, but may be of any color if not used in match play. Only club insignia, name of club, name of racquetball organization, name of tournament, or name of sponsor may be on the uniform. Players may not play without shirts.

PART III. OFFICIATING

Rule 3.1—Tournaments. All tournaments shall be managed by a committee or chairman, who shall designate the officials.

Rule 3.2—Officials. The officials shall include:

(a) A referee for all matches.

(b) A referee and two linesmen for all quarter-final, semifinal, championship and third place matches.

(c) Additional officials, assistants, score-keepers or record keepers may be designated as desired.

Rule 3.3—Qualifications. All officials shall be experienced or trained, and shall be thoroughly familiar with these rules and with the local playing conditions.

Rule 3.4—Briefing. Before each match the officials and players shall be briefed on rules and on local court hinders or other regulations.

Rule 3.5—Referees.

(a) **Pre-Match Duties.** Before each match commences, it shall be the duty of the referee to:

(1) Check on adequacy of preparation of the court with respect to cleanliness, lighting and temperature.

(2) Check on availability and suitability of all materials necessary for the match such as balls, towels, score cards and pencils.

(3) Check readiness and qualifications of assisting officials.

(4) Explain court regulations to players and inspect the compliance of racquets with rules upon request.

(5) Remind players to have an adequate supply of extra racquets and uniforms.

(6) Introduce players, toss coin, and signal start of first game.

(b) **Decisions.** During games the referee shall decide all questions that may arise in accordance with these rules. In National events (i.e., pro tour, regionals, National Championships, National Juniors or any other event deemed "National" by the USRA or NRC, a protest shall be decided by the National Director, or in his absence the National Commissioner, or in his absence the National Coordinator, or any other person delegated by the National Director. On all questions involving judgment and on all questions not covered by these rules, the decision of the referee is final.

(c) **Protests.** Any decision not involving the judgment of the referee may on protest be decided by the chairman, if present, or his delegated representative.

(d) **Forfeitures.** A match may be forfeited by the referee when:

(1) Any player refuses to abide by the referee's decision, or engages in unsportsmanlike conduct.

(2) After warning, any player leaves the court without permission of the referee during a game.

(3) Any player for a singles match, or any team for a doubles match fails to report to play. Normally, 20 minutes from the scheduled game time will be allowed before forfeiture. The tournament chairman may permit a longer delay if circumstances warrant such a decision.

(4) If any player for a singles or any team for a doubles fail to appear to play any matches or play-offs, they shall forfeit their ratings for future tournaments and forfeit any trophies, medals, awards or prize money.

(e) **"Referee's Technical."** The referee is empowered, after giving due warning, to deduct one point from a contestant's or his team's total score when in the referee's sole judgment, the contestant during the course of the match is being overtly and deliberately abusive beyond a point of reason. The warning referred to will be called a **"Technical Warning"** and the actual invoking of this penalty is called a **"Referee's Technical."** If after the technical is called against the abusing contestant and the play is not immediately continued within the alloted time provided for under the existing rules, the referee is empowered to forfeit the match in favor of the abusing contestant's opponent or opponents as the case may be. The **"Referee's Technical"** can be invoked by the referee as many times during the course of a match as he deems necessary.

(f) **Profanity.** No warning need be given by the referee, and an immediate "Referee's Technical" may be invoked by the referee if a player utters profane language in any way.

Rule 3.6—Scorers. The scorer may keep a record of the progress of the game in the manner prescribed by the committee or chairman. As a minimum the progress record shall include the order of serves, timeouts, and points. The referee may at his discretion also serve as scorer.

Rule 3.7—Record Keepers. In addition to the scorer, the committee may designate additional persons to keep more detailed records for statistical purposes of the progress of the game.

Rule 3.8—Linesmen. Two linesmen will be designated by the tournament chairman or referee and shall, at the referee's signal, either agree or disagree with the referee's ruling.

The official signal by a linesman to show agreement with the referee is "thumbs up." The official signal to show disagreement is "thumbs down." The official signal for no opinion is an "open palm down."

If both linesmen disagree with the referee, the referee must reverse his ruling. If one linesman agrees and one linesman disagrees or has no opinion the referee's call shall stand. If one linesman disagrees and one linesman has no opinion, the rally shall be replayed.

Rule 3.9—Appeals. In any match using linesmen, a player or team may appeal certain calls by the referee. These calls are

(1) kill shots (whether good or bad);
(2) fault serves; and
(3) double bounce pick-ups. At no time may a player or team appeal hinder, avoidable hinder or technical foul calls.

The appeal must be directed to the referee, who will then request opinions from the linesmen. Any appeal made directly to a linesman by a player or team will be considered null and void, and forfeit any appeal rights for that player or for that particular rally.

(a) **Kill-Shot Appeals.** If the referee makes a call of "good" on a kill shot attempt which ends a particular rally, the loser of the rally may appeal the call, if he feels the shot was not good. If the appeal is successful and the referee's original call reversed, the player who originally lost the rally is declared winner of the rally and is entitled to every benefit under the rules, i.e., point and/or service.

If the referee makes a call of "bad" or "skip" on a kill shot attempt, he has ended the rally. The player against whom the call went has the right to appeal the call, if he feels the shot was good. If the appeal is successful and the referee's original call reversed, the player who originally lost the rally is declared winner of the rally and is entitled to every benefit under the rules as winner of a rally.

(b) **Fault Serve Appeals.** If the referee makes a call of "fault" on a serve that the server felt was good, the server may appeal the call. If his appeal is successful, the server is then entitled to two additional serves.

If the served ball was considered by the referee to be an ace and in his opinion there was absolutely no way for the receiver to return the serve, then a point shall be awarded to the server.

If the referee makes a "no call" on a particular serve (therefore making it a legal serve) but either player feels the serve was short, either player may appeal the call at the end of the rally. If the loser of the rally appeals and wins his appeal, then the situation reverts back to the point of service with the call becoming fault. If it was a first service, one more serve attempt is allowed. If the server already had one fault, the second fault would cause a side out.

(c) **Double Bounce Pick-up Appeals.** If the referee makes a call of "two bounces," thereby stopping play, the player against whom the call was made has the right of appeal, if he feels he retrieved the ball legally. If the appeal is upheld, the rally is replayed.

If the referee makes no call on a particular play during the course of a rally in which one player feels his opponent retrieved a ball on two or more bounces, the player feeling this way has the right of appeal. However, since the ball is in play, the player wishing to appeal must clearly motion the referee

and linesmen by raising his non-racquet hand, thereby alerting them to the exact play which is being appealed. At the same time, the player appealing must continue to retrieve and play the rally.

If the appealing player should win the rally, no appeal is necessary. If he loses the rally, and his appeal is upheld, the call is reversed and the "good" retrieve by his oponent becomes a "double bounce pick-up," making the appealing player the winner of the rally and entitled to all benefits thereof.

Rule 3.10—If at any time during the course of a match the referee is of the opinion that a player or team is deliberately abusing the right of appeal, by either repetitious appeals of obvious rulings, or as a means of unsportsmanlike conduct, the referee shall enforce the Technical Foul rule.

PART IV. PLAY REGULATIONS

Rule 4.1—Serve—Generally.

(a) **Order.** The player or side winning the toss becomes the first server and starts the first game. The loser of the toss will serve first in the second game. The player or team scoring more points in games one and two combined shall serve first in the tie-breaker. In the event that both players or teams score an equal number of points in the first two games, another coin toss shall be held prior to the tie-breaker with the winner of the toss serving first.

(b) **Start.** Games are started from any point within the service zone. No part of either foot may extend beyond either line of the service zone. Stepping on the line (but not beyond it) is permitted. Server must remain in the service zone until the served ball passes the short line. Violations are called "foot faults."

(c) **Manner.** A serve is commenced by bouncing the ball to the floor in the service zone, and on the first bounce the ball is struck by the server's racquet so that it hits the front wall and on the rebound hits the floor back of the short line, either with or without touching one of the side walls.

(d) Readiness. Serves shall not be made until the receiving side is ready, or the referee has called play ball.

(e) Deliberate Delays. Deliberate delays on the part of the server or receiver exceeding 10 seconds shall result in an out or point against the offender.

(1) This "10-second rule" is applicable to both server and receiver, each of whom is allowed up to 10 seconds to serve or be ready to receive. It is the server's responsibility to look and be certain the receiver is ready. If the receiver is not ready, he must signal so by raising his racquet above his head. Such raising of the racquet is the only legal signal that the receiver may make to alert the referee and server that he is not ready.

(2) If the server serves a ball while the receiver is signaling "not ready" the serve shall go over with no penalty.

(3) If the server looks at the receiver and the receiver is not signaling "not readiness" the server may then serve. If the receiver attempts to signal "not ready" after this point such signal shall not be acknowledged and the serve becomes legal.

(f) Time-Outs. At no time shall a call of "time-out" by a player be acknowledged by the referee if the "time-out" call does not precede the serve, i.e., the so-called "Chabot time-out," is not legal. The beginning of the serve, as indicated in rule 4.1 c, is with the bounce of the ball.

Rule 4.2—Serve—In Doubles.

(a) Server. At the beginning of each game in doubles, each side shall inform the referee of the order of service which order shall be followed throughout the game. Only the first server serves the first time up and continues to serve first throughout the game. When the first server is out—the side is out. Thereafter both players on each side shall serve until a hand-out occurs. It is not necessary for the server to alternate serves to their opponents.

(b) Partner's Position. On each serve, the server's partner shall stand erect with his back to the side wall and with both feet on the floor within the service box until the served ball passes the short line. Violations are called "foot faults" subject to penalties thereof.

Rule 4.3—Defective Serves. Defective serves are of three types resulting in penalties as follows:

(a) Dead Ball Serve. A dead ball serve results in no penalty and the server is given another serve without cancelling a prior illegal serve.

(b) Fault Serve. Two fault serves result in a hand-out.

(c) Out Serves. An out serve results in a hand-out.

Rule 4.4—Dead Ball Serves. Dead ball serves do not cancel any previous illegal serve. They occur when an otherwise legal serve:

(a) Hits Partner. Hits the server's partner on the fly on the rebound from the front wall while the server's partner is in the service box. Any serve that touches the floor before hitting the partner in the box is a short.

(b) Screen Balls. Passes too close to the server or the server's partner to obstruct the view of the returning side. Any serve passing behind the server's partner and the side wall is an automatic screen.

(c) Court Hinders. Hits any part of the court that under local rules is a dead ball.

Rule 4.5—Fault Serves. The following serves are faults and any two in succession results in a hand-out:

(a) Foot Faults. A foot fault results:

(1) When the server leaves the service zone before the served ball passes the short line.

(2) When the server's partner leaves the service box before the served ball passes the short line.

(b) Short Service. A short service is any served ball that first hits the front wall and on the rebound hits the floor in front of the back edge of the short line either with or without touching one side wall.

(c) Three-Wall Serve. A three-wall serve is any ball served that first hits the front wall and on the rebound hits two side walls on the fly.

(d) Ceiling Serve. A ceiling serve is any served ball that touches the ceiling after hitting the front wall either with or without touching one side wall.

(e) Long Serve. A long serve is any served ball that first hits the front wall and rebounds to the back wall before touching the floor.

(f) Out of Court Serve. Any ball going out of the court on the serve.

Rule 4.6—Out Serves. Any one of the following serves results in a hand-out:

(a) A serve in which the ball is struck after being bounced outside the service zone.

(b) Missed Ball. Any attempt to strike the ball on the first bounce that results either in a total miss or in touching any part of the server's body other than his racquet.

(c) Non-Front Serve. Any served ball that strikes the server's partner, or the ceiling, floor or side wall, before striking the front wall.

(d) Touched Serve. Any served ball that on the rebound from the front wall touches the server or touches the server's partner while any part of his body is out of the service box or the server's partner intentionally catches the served ball on the fly.

(e) Out-of-Order Serve. In doubles, when either partner serves out of order.

(f) Crotch Serve. If the served ball hits the crotch in the front wall it is considered the same as hitting the floor and is an out. A crotch serve into the back wall (or side wall on three wall serves) is good and in play.

Rule 4.7—Return of Serve.

(a) The receiver or receivers may not infringe on the "five-foot zone" until the server strikes the ball. The receiver may then "rush" the serve and return it after the served ball passes the short line, as long as no part of the receiver's body or racquet breaks the plane of the service zone.

(b) Defective Serve. To eliminate any misunderstanding, the receiving side should not catch or touch a defectively served ball until called by the referee or it has touched the floor the second time.

(c) Fly Return. In making a fly return the receiver must end up with both feet back of the service zone. A violation by a receiver results in a point for the server.

(d) Legal Return. After the ball is legally served, one of the players on the receiving side must strike the ball with his racquet either on the fly or after the first bounce and before the ball touches the floor the second time to return the ball to the front wall either directly or after touching one or both side walls, the back wall or the ceiling, or any combination of those surfaces. A returned ball may not touch the floor before touching the front wall.

(1) It is legal to return the ball by striking the ball into the back wall first, then hitting the front wall on the fly or after hitting the side wall or ceiling.

(2) If the ball should strike the front wall, then back wall and then front wall again without striking the floor, the player whose turn it is to strike the ball, may do so by letting the ball bounce after hitting the front wall a second time.

(3) If the ball strikes the front wall, then back wall, and then front wall again after striking the floor, the player whose turn it is to strike the ball must do so by striking it before it hits the floor a second time.

(e) Failure to Return. The failure to return a serve results in a point for the server.

Rule 4.8—Changes of Serve.

(a) Hand-out. A server is entitled to continue serving until:

(1) Out Serve. He makes an out serve under Rule 4.6, or

(2) Fault Serves. He makes two fault serves in succession under Rule 4.5, or

(3) Hits Partner. He hits his partner with an attempted return, or

(4) Return Failure. He or his partner fails to keep the ball in play by returning it as required by Rule 4.7 (d), or

(5) Avoidable Hinder. He or his partner commits an avoidable hinder under Rule 4.11.

(b) Side-out

(1) In Singles. In singles, retiring the server retires the side.

(2) In Doubles. In doubles, the side is retired when both partners have been

put out, except on the first serve as provided in Rule 4.2 (a).

(c) **Effect.** When the server or the side loses the serve, the server or serving side shall become the receiver; and the receiver or receiving side, the server; and so alternately in all subsequent services of the game.

Rule 4.9—Rallies. Each legal return after the serve is called a rally. Play during rallies shall be according to the following rules:

(a) **One or Both Hands.** Only the head of the racquet may be used at any time to return the ball. The ball must be hit with the racquet in one or both hands. Switching hands to hit a ball is an out. The use of any portion of the body is an out.

(b) **One Touch.** In attempting returns, the ball may be touched only once by one player on returning side. In doubles both partners may swing at, but only one may hit the ball. Each violation of (a) or (b) results in a handout or point.

(c) **Return Attempts.**

(1) In Singles. In singles if a player swings at but misses the ball in play, the player may repeat his attempts to return the ball until it touches the floor the second time.

(2) In Doubles. In doubles if one player swings at but misses the ball, both he and his partner may make further attempts to return the ball until it touches the floor the second time. Both partners on a side are entitled to an attempt to return the ball.

(3) Hinders. In singles or doubles, if a player swings at but misses the ball in play and in his or his partner's attempt again to play the ball there is an unintentional interference by an opponent it shall be a hinder. See Rule 4.10.

(d) **Touching Ball.** Except as provided in Rule 4.10 (a) (2), any touching of a ball before it touches the floor the second time by a player other than the one making a return is a point or out against the offending player.

(e) **Out of Court Ball.**

(1) After Return. Any ball returned to the front wall which on the rebound or on the first bounce goes into the gallery or through any opening in a side wall shall be declared dead and the serve replayed.

(2) No Return. Any ball not returned to the front wall, but which caroms off a player's racquet into the gallery or into any opening in a side wall either with or without touching the ceiling, side or back wall, shall be an out or point against the player or players failing to make the return.

(f) **Dry Ball.** During the game and particularly on service every effort should be made to keep the ball dry. Deliberate wetting shall result in an out.

(g) **Broken Ball.** If there is any suspicion that the ball has broken during the serve, or during a rally, play shall continue until the end of the rally. The referee or any player may request the ball be examined. If the referee decides the ball is broken or otherwise defective, a new ball shall be put into play and the rally replayed.

(h) **Ball Inspection.** The ball may be inspected by the referee between rallies at any time during a match.

(i) **Play Stoppage.**

(1) If a player loses a shoe or other equipment, or foreign objects enter the court, or any other outside interference occurs, the referee shall stop the play.

(2) Players wearing protective eye glasses have the responsibility of having such eye glasses securely fastened. In the event that such protective eye glasses should become unfastened and enter the court, the play shall be stopped as long as such eye glasses were fastened initially. In the event such eye glasses are not securely fastened, no stoppage of play shall result and the player wearing such glasses plays at his own risk.

(3) If a player loses control of his racquet, time should be called after the point has been decided, providing the racquet does not strike an opponent or interfere with ensuing play.

Rule 4.10—Dead Ball Hinders. Hinders are of two types—"dead ball" and "avoidable." Dead ball hinders as described in this rule result in the rally being replayed. Avoidable hinders are described in Rule 4.11.

(a) Situations. When called by the referee, the following are dead ball hinders:

(1) Court Hinders. Hits any part of the court which under local rules is a dead ball.

(2) Hitting Opponent. Any returned ball that touches an opponent on the fly before it returns to the front wall.

(3) Body Contact. Any body contact with an opponent that interferes with seeing or returning the ball.

(4) Screen Ball. Any ball rebounding from the front wall close to the body of a player on the side which just returned the ball to interfere with or prevent the returning side from seeing the ball. See Rule 4.4 (b).

(5) Straddle Ball. A ball passing between the legs of a player on the side which just returned the ball, if there is no fair chance to see or return the ball.

(6) Back Swing Hinder. If there is body contact on the back swing, the player must call it immediately. This is the only hinder call a player can make.

(7) Other Interference. Any other unintentional interference which prevents an opponent from having a fair chance to see or return the ball.

(b) Effect. A call by the referee of a "hinder" stops the play and voids any situation following such as the ball hitting a player. No player is authorized to call a hinder, except on the back swing and such a call must be made immediately, as provided in Rule 4.10 (a) (6).

(c) Avoidance. While making an attempt to return the ball, a player is entitled to a fair chance to see and return the ball. It is the duty of the side that has just served or returned the ball to move so that the receiving side may go straight to the ball and not be required to go around an opponent. The referee should be liberal in calling hinders to discourage any practice of playing the ball where an adversary cannot see it until too late. It is no excuse that the ball is "killed," unless in the opinion of the referee the ball couldn't be returned. Hinders should be called without a claim by a player, especially in close plays and on game points.

(d) In Doubles. In doubles, both players on a side are entitled to a fair and unobstructed chance at the ball and either one is entitled to a hinder even though naturally it would be his partner's ball and even though his partner may have attempted to play the ball or that he may already have missed it. It is not a hinder when one player hinders his partner.

Rule 4.11—Avoidable Hinders. An avoidable hinder results in an "out" or a point depending upon whether the offender was serving or receiving.

(a) Failure to Move. Does not move sufficiently to allow opponent his shot.

(b) Blocking. Moves into a position effecting a block, on the opponent about to return the ball, or, in doubles, one partner moves in front of an opponent as his partner is returning the ball.

(c) Moving into Ball. Moves in the way and is struck by the ball just played by his opponent.

(d) Pushing. Deliberately pushing or shoving an opponent during a rally.

Rule 4.12—Rest Periods.

(a) Delays. Deliberate delay exceeding 10 seconds by server, or receiver, shall result in an out or point against the offender. [See Rule 4.1 (e).]

(b) During Game. During a game each player in singles, or each side in doubles, either while serving or receiving may request a "time-out" for a towel, wiping glasses, change or adjustment. Each "time-out" shall not exceed 30 seconds. No more than three "time-outs" in a game shall be granted each singles player or each team in doubles. Two "time-outs" shall be allotted each player in singles or each team in doubles in the tie-breaker.

(c) Injury. No time shall be charged to a player who is injured during play. An injured player shall not be allowed more than a total of 15 minutes of rest. If the injured player is not able to resume play after total rests of 15 minutes the match shall be awarded to the opponent or opponents. On any further injury to same player, the Tournament Director, if present, or committee after considering any available medical opinion shall determine whether the injured player will be allowed to continue.

(d) Between Games. A five-minute rest period is allowed between the first and second games and a five-minute rest period between the second and third games. Players may leave the court between games, but must be on the court and ready to play at the expiration of the rest period.

(e) Postponed Games. Any games postponed by referee due to weather elements shall be resumed with the same score as when postponed.

Glossary

"A" player—player whose skill level is very high. Sometimes used synonymously with the term *open player*. Varies locally.

Ace—a serve that wins the point outright without receiver return.

Add-on—one of a series of links or small movements that combine to form one continuous chain or larger motion.

Anticipation—the art and science of predicting where an opponent is going to hit the ball.

Appeal—the call for further judgment when one player disagrees with the referee's call. For example, a player may appeal a shot that he thought was good but which the referee called a skip. If both linesmen disagree with the ref's call, that call is overruled. If one or both linesmen agree with the referee, the call is upheld.

Around-the-wall ball—a defensive shot from the old days of control racquetball. The ball hits high on one sidewall, then the front wall, then the opposite sidewall before finally bouncing on the floor in deep court.

Avoidable hinder—an interference or hinder, sometimes intentional and sometimes not, which hampers the flow of play. For example, stepping in front of an opponent's shot. Results in either a side-out or a point.

"B" player—player whose skill level is average. Varies locally.

Back court—that court area between the short line and the back wall.

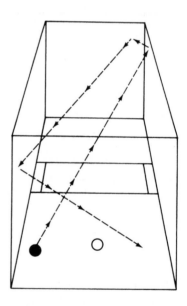

Around-the-wall ball. A defensive shot from the old days of control racquetball. The ball hits high on one sidewall, then the front wall, then the opposite sidewall, before finally bouncing on the floor in deep court.

Backhand—one of the two fundamental strokes. This is hit on the side of the body opposite the hand with which one holds the racquet.

Backhand corner—this may be either the front or the rear backhand corner. It is the court area on the player's backhand side.

Backhand grip—the way the hand grasps the racquet for the backhand stroke.

Ball-into-back-wall shot—a ball driven into the rear wall, which then travels in the air to the front wall. This is a strategically weak shot.

Back spin—ball rotation that has reverse or bottom spin. Results from hitting with the racquet angled in an open face.

Backswing—the preparatory part of a stroke in which the racquet is taken back to the ready position.

Back wall—the rear wall. This is forty feet from and parallel to the front wall.

Back wall shot—any ball hit after a rebound off the back wall.

Block—a hinder, avoidable or unavoidable, resulting from one player getting in front of the other player during the latter's shot.

Bottom board—the imaginary strip or board across the bottom of the front wall from sidewall to sidewall. This is the target area for kill shots—low on the front wall. A bottom boarder is therefore a kill shot that rolls off the bottom board of the front wall.

Bumper—the protective strip of material on the head of many metal racquets. This protects the racquet and walls, as well as providing additional head weight.

Butt—the enlarged end bump at the bottom of the racquet handle. This helps prevent grip slippage.

"C" player—player whose skill level is considered novice. This is usually the novice or lowest class event in a tournament. Varies locally.

Ceiling ball—the most common defensive shot. The struck ball hits the ceiling near the front wall, strikes the front wall, then rebounds off the floor with a high bounce toward the back wall.

Ceiling serve—a serve that hits the ceiling either before or after front wall contact. The former is a side-out and the latter only a fault.

Center court—the court area near the service box, which is strategically important during rallies.

Choke—(1) to move the hand up or down on the racquet handle; (2) to psych out in a match.

Closed face—a racquet face angle whereby the strong surface slants toward the floor. Usually causes the ball to skip into the floor.

Cock position—the ready position for the wrist

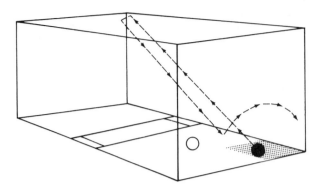

Ceiling ball. The most common defensive shot. The struck ball hits the ceiling near the front wall, strikes the front wall, then rebounds on the floor with a high bounce toward the back wall.

in preparation for hitting the ball. The wrist is subsequently snapped at ball contact.

Contact zone—the area in which the ball is normally hit with the racquet. Ideally, the point of contact is in the exact center of a player's contact zone.

Control—the ability to consistently place the ball in the court in a premeditated manner.

Control player—a player whose game strategy revolves around hitting control shots to earn points.

Corner shot—a kill that hits near one of the two front corners.

Court hinder—an unavoidable hinder brought about by an obstacle in the court. For example, the ball hitting a door latch and taking a strange bounce. Play goes over.

Crack shot—a ball that hits in the crack juncture between the floor and the side or rear wall.

Cross-court pass—a pass shot hit from the left side of the court to the right, or from the right to the left. Also called a V-ball.

Crotch—the line juncture at which two flat surfaces of the court join. For example, the floor-sidewall crotch.

Crotch shot—any shot that strikes right in the juncture between the floor and any wall of the court.

Cutthroat—a form of racquetball in which three players participate. Each player during her serve scores points and plays against the other two players.

Defensive player—the covering player whose

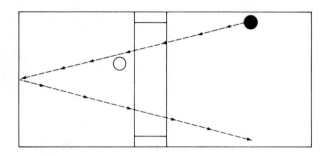

Crosscourt pass. A pass shot hit from the left side of the court to the right, or from the right to left. Also called a V-ball.

turn it is not to hit the next shot during a rally.

Dead Ball—(1) any shot that stops play due to a hinder call or to the ball flying out of the court; (2) a racquetball that is slow, or does not bounce as high as usual (a relative term).

Defensive shot—a type of shot whose purpose is generally to continue the rally rather than end it. The three main defensive shots are the ceiling ball, Z-ball, and around-the-wall ball.

Donut—zero points. To beat an opponent 21–0 is to give her the donut.

Doubles—a form of racquetball in which two teams composed of two players each compete.

Downswing—the forward and downward motion of the racquet from the top of the backswing to the point of contact.

Down-the-line pass—a pass shot hit from near either the left or the right sidewall that travels directly to the front wall, then rebounds straight back along the sidewall of origin.

Drive serve—the most offensive serve. This is hit low into the front wall and rebounds low and hard into either of the rear court corners.

English—another term for the spin imparted to a ball by the racquet.

Error, mental—to commit a cerebral blunder as in making a poor choice of shot selection.

Error, physical—to mis-hit a normally playable shot, as in skipping in an easy setup.

Exchange—the change in positions of the two players following the end of a rally. The server becomes the receiver, and vice versa.

Face—the hitting surface of the racquet; the plane formed by the racquet strings.

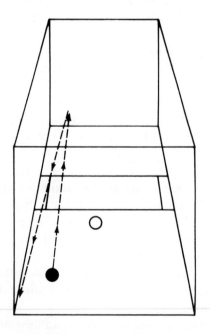

Down-the-line pass. A pass shot hit from near either the left or right sidewall, which travels directly to the front wall, then rebounds straight back along the sidewall of origin.

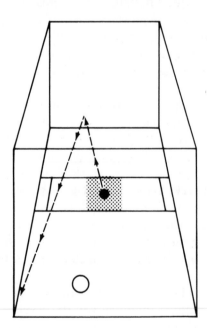

Drive serve. The most offensive serve. This is hit low into the front wall and rebounds low and hard into either of the rear court corners.

Fault—an illegal serve or a foot fault that gives the server his second and last opportunity to put the ball into play legally; for example, a long serve.

Five-foot line—the short red line on the floor or sidewall five feet behind the short line of the service box. This line concerns the five-foot rule.

Five-foot rule—a safety regulation that states that (1) the receiver must begin by standing behind the five-foot line to receive the serve; and (2) the receiver may not cross the vertical plane above the five-foot line when returning any serve before it hits the floor—on the fly.

Fly ball—any shot taken before a floor bounce, directly on the rebound off the front or sidewall; also called a volley shot.

Follow-through—the continuation of the forehand or backhand stroke after ball contact.

Foot fault—the illegal placement of one or both of the server's feet on either the service line or the short line during the service motion.

Footwork—the movement of the feet during play; usually denotes foot movement while setting up to hit a shot.

Forehand—one of the two basic strokes in racquetball, in which the ball is hit on the side of the body where the hitting arm is located.

Forehand corner—the front or rear quadrant of the court on the side where the player hits forehand shots.

Forehand grip—the manner in which a player grasps the racquet to hit forehand shots.

Four-wall racquetball—the most popular variety of the game, as opposed to three-wall or one-wall. In this, the ball is played off the four walls, the ceiling, and the floor.

Front-and-back—one method of dividing court coverage responsibilities between the two players of one doubles team. An imaginary line is drawn from sidewall to sidewall; one player covers the front court and the other the back court. (*See also* **Half-and-half.**)

Front court—that area of the court nearer the front wall; usually defined as the court surface in front of and including the service box.

Front wall kill—any kill shot that is hit straight into the front wall without prior sidewall contact.

Game—one racquetball contest. The game is to

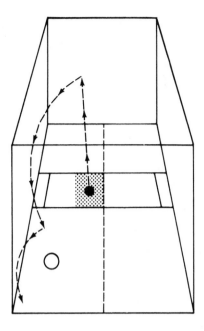

Garbage serve. A half-speed serve that hits midway up the front wall and presents itself to the receiver at near shoulder height in either of the rear court corners.

twenty-one points, and a player need win by only one point to take a game.

Gamesmanship—the use of unusual, dubious, or psychological tactics on or off the court to gain a winning edge.

Garbage serve—a half-speed serve that hits midway up on the front wall and presents itself to the receiver at near shoulder height in either of the rear court corners.

Grip—(1) the manner in which the racquet handle is grasped; (2) the cover material of the racquet handle that prevents slippage.

Gun hand—the hand that a player uses to grip the racquet.

Half-and-half—the most common method of dividing the court coverage responsibilities between the two members of one doubles team. An imaginary line is drawn down the center of the court from the front to back walls; one player covers shots on the right side, the other balls on the left side. (*See also* **Front-and-back.**)

Half-volley—to hit the ball on the short hop, or just after it bounces on the floor.

Hand-out—the loss of service by one player of a doubles team. It then becomes her partner's

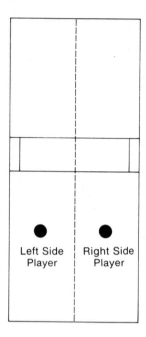

Half and half. The most common method of dividing the court coverage responsibilities between the two members of one doubles team. In this, an imaginary line is drawn down the center of the court from the front to the back walls. One player covers shots on the right side, the other the left side.

turn to serve. Two hand-outs make a side-out, which means the opposing team gains the service.

Handshake grip—the most common method of gripping the racquet, in which the handle is basically grasped as though shaking hands with a person.

Head—the hitting surface of the racquet, including the rim and strung face.

Hypotenuse shot—a kill shot that travels from one rear corner to the opposite front corner.

I-formation—the same as the front-and-back formation in doubles.

Inning—a round of play in singles in which both players have served, or in doubles in which both players of each team have served.

Isolation strategy—a strategy in doubles by which one team isolates one player of the opposing team by hitting the majority of serves and shots to her. The intent is to tire out the isolated player, while letting the other team member get cold due to lack of play.

Kill shot—a shot that hits so low on the front wall that its low rebound makes it irretrievable; also called a kill.

Let—any interruption of play; for example, a hinder or screen ball.

Linesmen—the two referee's aides who are called upon to judge an appeal call made by one of the players.

Live ball—(1) a ball that is still in play, as opposed to a dead ball; (2) a racquetball that is fast or has a high bounce (a relative term).

Lob—(1) an infrequently used serve that drops from a high arc into one of the rear corners; (2) an infrequently used defensive shot that is hit high and usually crosscourt into one of the rear corners.

Long serve—any served ball that carries on the fly to the back wall; this is an illegal serve and counts as one fault.

Match—a complete racquetball contest composed of the best two out of three games. The first two games are to twenty-one points and the third, if necessary, is usually a tiebreaker to eleven points.

Mercy ball—a special situation that is governed by an unwritten rule of court etiquette and safety. It occurs when one player holds up her swing because, had she instead hit the ball, that shot or her racquet probably would have struck the opponent. This is a simple hinder and the play goes over.

Model stroke—the universal stroke, or the swing learned quickest by the most number of players with the best possible results.

Non-front wall serve—any serve that initially strikes any surface other than the front wall; the serve is illegal and results in a side-out.

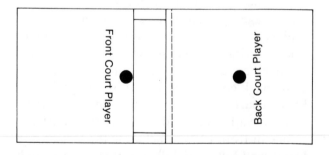

I-formation. The same as the front-and-back formation in doubles. In this, an imaginary line is drawn from sidewall to sidewall. One player covers the front court and the other the back court.

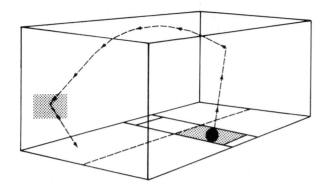

Lob. (1) An infrequently used serve that drops from a high arc into one of the rear corners. (2) An infrequently used defensive shot that is hit high and usually crosscourt into one of the rear corners.

Novice—a relatively low-skilled player, or a beginner at the sport; sometimes synonymous with "C" player.

Offensive player—the player whose turn it is to hit the ball.

Offensive shot—any shot intended either to end the rally immediately or to put the opponent in a weak court position; usually a kill or pass shot.

Offhand—the non-gun hand, or the one that doesn't grasp the racquet.

One-grip system—one method of grasping the racquet by which the same grip is used for both the forehand and backhand strokes.

One-on-two—a hybrid combination of singles and doubles in which a strong player plays against a team of two players. The single player may take two serves or, as an additional handicap, may take only one serve to the team's usual two.

One-wall racquetball—an outdoor variety of the sport in which only a front wall is utilized. Lines on the floor mark the remainder of the playing area.

Open face—the angle of the racquet upon ball contact such that the hitting surface is slanted toward the ceiling; this causes unwanted slicing or back spin on the ball.

Overhead—any shot that is struck with an overhand or baseball throwing motion. Includes the overhead pass and overhead kill.

Overruled—the concurrent decision by the two linesmen to reverse the original appealed call by the referee.

Paddleball—racquetball's immediate predecessor, which has the same court and rules but uses a wooden paddle and deader ball.

Paralysis via analysis—to freeze or choke mentally due to overanalyzing a shot or stroke.

Pass shot—a shot hit past an opponent either to gain an immediate point or to put the opponent out of position. May be cross court or down the line. Also called a drive shot.

Pinch shot—a type of kill shot that glances off the sidewall into the front wall. A kill to the sidewall first.

Point—the unit of scoring in racquetball. Only the server may score a point by winning the rally—the receiver gains a side-out if she wins the rally. Also called a tally.

Portsider—a left-handed player; a southpaw.

Psych out—(1) to gain a mental edge over an opponent through the use of psychological ploys; (2) to falter mentally and blow a shot or match that should have been a sure thing.

Psych up—to prepare mentally before or during a match.

Rally—the time between the serve and the error during which the ball is in play.

Ready position—(1) the stance taken by the receiver just before the ball is served; (2) the set position of a player waiting for the ball to drop into her contact zone.

Receiver—the player to whom the serve is hit.

Receiving line—the five-foot line.

Referee—the person who oversees a tournament match; the referee frequently doubles as the scorekeeper.

Referee's elbow—the buildup of calluses on the elbows brought about by leaning on those elbows while refereeing many games; also called Steding's elbow.

Reverse corner kill—a kill shot hit crosscourt into the far front corner.

Rim—the frame of a racquet. The most common materials for a frame are fiberglass (plastic), aluminum (metal), graphite (composite), and wood (laminated).

Rollout—a kill shot that comes low and flat off the front wall. This is usually irretrievable and scores a point or a side-out.

Safety hinder—the interruption of a rally because ensuing play could cause an injury. It results simply in playing the rally over; for

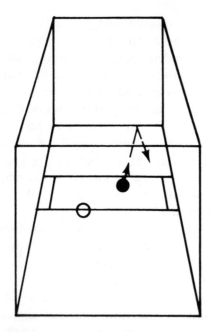

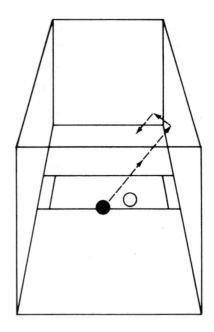

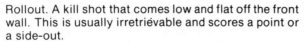

Rollout. A kill shot that comes low and flat off the front wall. This is usually irretrievable and scores a point or a side-out.

Sidewall–front wall kill shot. Another term for the pinch kill. A kill into the sidewall first.

example, a mercy ball or a foreign object falling onto the court.

Serve—(1) the ball hit by the server, which initiates a rally, also called a service; (2) the act of putting such a ball into play.

Server—the player who serves or hits the first ball of the rally.

Serve return—the shot used to return the served ball.

Service box—the area from which the server serves. This is marked on the sides by the two sidewalls, on the front by the service line, and on the back by the short line.

Set position—the ready position or the initial stance assumed by a player about to hit the ball.

Set-up—(1) to prepare for a swing via footwork and a backswing; (2) a potential shot during the rally that should be an easy scoring opportunity for the hitter. Most setups are killed by better players (for example, a back wall setup).

Shooter—an aggressive player who adopts an attack strategy; his shot selection depends highly on the kill.

Shoot the ball—to attempt to kill the ball.

Short line—the back line of the service box that lies halfway between the front and back walls; served balls must carry beyond this line.

Side-by-side—another term for the half-and-half method of doubles coverage.

Sidewall–front wall kill shot—another term for the pinch kill; a kill to the sidewall first.

Singles—the most common form of racquetball, in which one player competes against another.

Southpaw—a left-handed player; portsider.

Spin—the intended or unintended English imparted to the ball by the racquet strings during the stroke.

Stall—to intentionally delay the progress of the game in order to recover physically or mentally, to psych out the other player, etc.

Straddleball—any shot that passes through the legs of one of the players after the front wall rebound; this is a hinder only if it visually or physically impedes the other player from hitting the ball.

Straight-in kill—another term for a front-wall-first kill shot.

Stroke—(1) the manner in which a player swings at the ball; a forehand or backhand; (2) the act of hitting a forehand or backhand.

Superpinch—a double sidewall kill shot that is usually an accident; the ball hits one sidewall, ricochets crosscourt into the opposite sidewall, then rolls off the front wall.

Sweet spot—the area of the racquet face that

provides the most control and power; generally the center of the strings, though the exact location depends on head shape, head weight, etc.

Tally—another term for a point.

Target area—the area on the front wall at which a serve or shot is aimed.

Technical—a rare call made by a referee during a tournament, usually for unsportsmanlike conduct such as swearing or stalling. The guilty player has one point subtracted from her score.

Tension—the amount of pressure with which a racquet is strung; normally twenty-two to thirty pounds.

Thong—the loop of cord tethered to the racquet butt, which the player wraps around her wrist as a safety precaution to keep the racquet from flying from her fist.

Three-wall racquetball—an outdoor variety of the sport in which a front and two partial or full sidewalls are utilized; the back wall is replaced by a line on the playing surface.

Three-wall serve—an illegal serve that strikes three walls before hitting the floor—front wall, sidewall, oposite sidewall; counts as one service fault.

Tie breaker—the third game of a match that is usually played to eleven points.

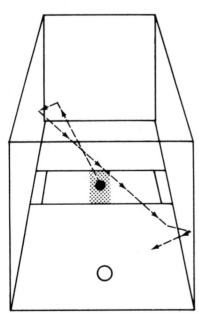

Z-serve (to the forehand). A multiangled, multiwalled serve to either the opponent's forehand or her backhand. The flight path is front wall, sidewall, floor, and then opposite sidewall.

Time-out—a legal break in play called for by one player or team. The length and number of time-outs allotted varies with the tournament or organization.

Top spin—the direction of ball rotation, usually caused by swinging with a closed face racquet.

Tournament—formal supervised play in which trophies, prizes, or money are often awarded the top finishers.

Trigger-finger grip—the proper method of grasping the racquet, which allows a small space between the middle and index fingers. This lets the hand cover more of the handle surface, thus providing more control. Also called the pistol grip.

Twinkie—One point; to beat an opponent 21-1 is to give her the twinkie.

Two-grip system—the more common method of grasping the racquet, in which a slightly different grip is used for the forehand and backhand strokes.

Unavoidable hinder—most often, intentional interference in the progress of play by one of the players; for example, purposefully blocking a shot. This results in either a side-out for the receiver or a point for the server.

V-ball—another term for a crosscourt pass or a V-pass.

Volley—to take the ball out of the air before a floor bounce. This is legal both on the serve return and during the rally. Also called a fly shot.

Waffle face—term used to describe the action of, or effect of, accidentally hitting a player in the face with the strung face of the racquet.

Wallpaper ball—a pass or ceiling shot that, en route from front to back wall, closely hugs a side wall.

Winner—a successful kill shot that results in a point or side-out.

Z-ball—a defensive shot used infrequently among higher ranks. This shot hits the front wall high in one corner, glances into the near sidewall, carries on the fly to the opposite sidewall, then hits the floor. The flight pattern traces the letter Z.

Z-serve—a multiangled, multiwalled serve to either the opponent's forehand or her backhand. The flight path is front wall, sidewall, floor, and then opposite sidewall.

Index

Other Books by Steve Keeley

Order from: Service Press, Inc.
              6369 Reynolds Rd.
              Haslett, MI 48840

The Complete Book of Racquetball: DBI Books, $7.95, instructional text.

Racquetball Lessons Made Easy: MacDonald Assoc., $7.95, instructional, two one-hour cassettes and booklet.

It's A Racquet!: Service Press, $3.95, racquetball anecdote book.

The Kill & Rekill Gang: Service Press, $4.95, racquetball cartoon book.

Racquetball 103—Beginners and *Racquetball 203—Advanced:* Strokeminder, $17.95 per set, instructional, each set includes three instant replay flipbooks and course material.